Dearest Roberta & Bob

Enjoy fun & Simple
Gourmet!

live well,
love well,
eat well...
XoXo
love you!
Gigi

Gigi STYLE
FUN & SIMPLE
GOURMET

Photography by Gerri (Gigi) Wilson

Book Design by David W. Myers, Dave Myers Design

Creative Collaboration and Editing Dana Rose, Mine Studios, LLC

Gigi Style ~ Fun & Simple Gourmet
Copyright 2016 @ by Gerri Wilson
www.gigiwilson.com

Published by Pinnacle SE Publishing Inc., 2016
Hilton Head Island, SC 29928
www.pinnaclesepublishing.com

Printed by Signature Book Printing
www.sbpbooks.com

GOURMET
what does it mean, really?

There are many definitions and interpretations, but from its French origin, the original term *"gourmet,"* was used to describe a wine broker or wine taster. Later, in the early 1800's, the first restaurant guide was produced in Paris characterizing *"gourmet"* as a connoisseur of fine food and drink. In the French liberal Encyclopedie, *"gourmet"* is defined as "one who possesses a refined and uncontrolled love of good food," synonymous with *"gastronome,"* one who appreciates good cuisine, in other words, quite simply, **one who appreciates good cooking.**

In Italy, this passion for food is sometimes called *una buona forchetta*, translated "a good fork," or *buongustaio*, which translates to gourmet in French. The English translation is just simply, *"**foodie**."* However it is described, *gourmet* is nothing more than enjoying food.

Welcome to **Gigi Style**~*the fun and simple world of Gigi's Gourmet Cuisine!*

a few words~

First, a word about good cuisine…*"FRESH."* There is just no other way…period. Fresh is essential to good cooking. Food doesn't have to be elaborate or complicated, it doesn't have to take all day to prepare, but it does have to start with fresh ingredients. Keep it simple, keep it fresh, this is what makes good food fabulous.

Second, a word about *"ORGANIC."* You will find most of my recipes list organic ingredients. Of course, organic is not necessary, but I do try to use as many organic ingredients as I can find for any dish. The main reasons to choose certified organic products are that they do not contain pesticides, additives, preservatives, MSG, or artificial sweeteners. In addition, organic farms are designed to reduce pollution and conserve water. Are organic foods more nutritious than fresh conventional foods? Probably not, but I am a fan of reducing chemicals and protecting our environment.

Third, a word about Olive Oil…okay, two words…*"LIQUID GOLD."* I use good olive oil in some variety in almost every recipe, even baking. There are so many wonderful olive oils from all over the world, various pressing processes, flavors, etc. Light, fruity, rich, spicy…finding a new wonderful olive oil is like discovering a new favorite bottle of wine. Olive Oil can be the very essence of almost any dish and it's healthy too! I tend to stay with extra virgin oils that are of a first cold pressed processing. The exception would be in baking when I generally use an extra light variety.

As Olive Oil is Liquid Gold, *freshly squeezed lemon* is *"LIQUID SUNSHINE,"* and together, they are a fabulous combination of healthy flavor enhancing freshness. You'll find this combination throughout the book in many of the recipes.

P.S. If you have a bottle of "Real Lemon" in your refrigerator, throw it away immediately. There is absolutely no substitute for fresh lemon.

LET'S TALK

About Seasoning I recommend always seasoning with good sea salt or kosher salt and freshly ground pepper. When it comes to spices, freshly ground dried spices have the best aromatics and therefore flavor. Most all specialty markets and even most supermarkets today have freshly ground spices available. Buy them in relatively small quantities as spices do not retain their intense flavors for long periods of time. Store in a cool dry place and never use after the expiration date. Spices that have been in your pantry for months (or years!) no longer have flavor, get rid of them immediately.

About Salt Salt enhances and opens the flavor of food. I love experimenting with fun sea salts of various origin, variety and color. For example, I enjoy a nice pink sea salt with a pink fish like salmon, red snapper or rainbow trout; or shell fish, like shrimp or lobster. Black sea salt is a great finish for a white flaky fish or poultry, enhancing flavor and adding color.

About Salads Probably the most versatile dish on any menu. Breakfast, lunch, dinner, side salads, entrée salads, fruit salads, vegetable salads, pasta/rice salads, seafood salads, meat and poultry salads…okay, enough already. You get my point, a salad goes with every meal or can be the meal. I like doing salads with lots of color and variety of flavors and textures that work well together. Turning a simple plate of lettuce into an extravagant and blissfully satisfying dining experience with fresh and healthy ingredients is just simply good stuff.

About Pasta My favorite comfort food, there is no denying it, or denying me! I love to make my own fresh pasta every chance I get, especially on weekends when there is more time, however, making pasta truly doesn't require a lot of time or even effort. I've never served a fresh pasta dish that hasn't been thoroughly enjoyed and totally devoured.

About Healthy Eating healthy doesn't mean giving up flavor or the foods you love. Most of the recipes in this book are derived from very healthy natural ingredients with reasonable portion sizes. Healthy eating is not sacrificing lifestyle, it is enhancing life. In addition, nearly all of the recipes can be prepared gluten-free simply by replacing the flour with "Cup 4 Cup" gluten-free flour, or any gluten-free flour of your choice.

About Presentation I consider an empty plate my canvas and every meal my little Picasso. It doesn't take much time or effort to make your presentation special whether it be in the way your arrange the food on a plate, or your table setting. Be creative and have fun with it!

All it takes is a little love…the secret ingredient for simple to spectacular!

Let's get cooking

Gigi STYLE

— the beautifully fun & simple gourmet way!

enjoy!

the beautifully
simple world of Gigi STYLE

FUN & SIMPLE
GOURMET

CONTENTS

GiGi Wilson

INTRODUCTION

It has been said that each one of us has God given talents, gifts that, if we are fortunate enough to become aware of, we are to embrace, learn from, practice, perfect, and share with others. I discovered at a very young age that I had a passion for cooking. Before I was tall enough to reach, I would push a chair from the kitchen table to the cooktop to scramble eggs for breakfast.

Though cooking is my passion, my gift is imagination and an incredible sense of taste and smell. I realized early that God gave me the ability to recognize flavors and develop combinations of flavors that worked well together, creating dishes that are not only pleasing to the palate and to the eye, but fun and easy to prepare in an elegantly basic way...from simple to spectacular!

I have put together a compilation of some of my favorites that I hope you will enjoy and share with those who you love.

A dear friend of mine once said, "Good food, good wine, great friends to share with, it doesn't get any better in this life." I tend to agree…

live well, love well, eat well!

*Gigi*STYLE   1

good mornin'

SUNSHINE!

breakfast
& BRUNCH

GREEN ON-THE-GO SMOOTHIE

makes one

I try to fill my day with healthy, energy packed fruits and vegetables. For a power packed breakfast or a quick lunch on the go, this combination green smoothie will get your engine running and keep you going throughout the day!

½ cup green grapes
½ medium banana
½ cup fresh pineapple chunks
2 cups fresh baby spinach leaves and
   stems, rinsed and dried

¼ cup water
6 large ice cubes
½ medium orange, peeled *(optional)*

Peel orange with a knife removing all white pith. Place in blender, I recommend a Vitamix. Follow with the grapes, banana, pineapple and spinach. Add water and secure the lid. Start blending on low speed, slowly increasing to the highest setting and blend until smooth. Place ice cubes on top of the mixture. Secure the lid and blend on high speed until the ice cubes have fully incorporated into the smoothie, approximately one minute or to desired consistency.

variation

½ cup green grapes
1 medium Hass avocado
½ cup fresh pineapple chunks
1 cup spinach leaves and stems

1 cup kale leaves *(stems removed)*
½ cup chopped carrots
¼ cup water
6 large ice cubes

Blend as directed above for this extra green fresh starter!

green

fruit smoothies!

TROPICAL MANGO SMOOTHIE

makes one

I love the sweetness and texture of a fresh mango. This smoothie doubles as a fresh morning starter, or a fabulous tropical daiquiri at cocktail time by adding a jigger of dark rum!

1 large fresh mango
1 medium orange, peeled
2 tablespoons simple syrup infused with mint leaves
5-6 large ice cubes

Cut mango with a Mango Splitter, which is an every kitchen must have item. (OXO makes a great one!) Discard the center seed portion. Holding one half of the mango in your hand skin side down, make slices across the flesh side being careful not to cut through the mango skin. Spoon the slices into the blender and do the same with the other half. Peel orange with a paring knife removing all white pith and add to the blender along with simple syrup. Place ice cubes on top. Secure the lid and blend until smooth, approximately one minute.

In a small saucepan, stir together 1 cup water and ½ cup sugar (I use organic cane sugar) with a wooden spoon over medium high heat until all sugar has dissolved, approximately 5 minutes. Remove from heat and stir in ¼ cup fresh mint leaves. Allow to rest until completely cooled, stirring a time or two during the infusion process. Discard mint leaves.

VERY BERRY SMOOTHIE

makes one

This morning starter is a berry lovers dream! No need for added sugar or dairy. The sweetness of the berries and creaminess of the banana are all you need for a perfectly healthy fruit smoothie. Simple and delicious.

1 medium banana
1 cup blueberries, strawberries, blackberries and/or raspberries
½ cup water
5-6 large ice cubes
Sprig of mint *(optional)*

Place fruit in blender. Pour water over fruit and place ice cubes on top. Secure the lid and start blending on low speed, slowly increasing to the highest setting. Blend until smooth. Top with a fresh sprig of mint if desired.

*If using frozen berries, use 1 cup water and no ice cubes.

PUMPKIN MUFFINS

One of the fun things about living in a resort community, is the constant flow of house guests. I always have fresh baked muffins in the freezer, to serve with fruit and coffee when our guests start their day. Pumpkin is my favorite. The soothing aroma of warm spices, cinnamon, nutmeg and cloves are a great way to wake up the senses and start any day.

3⅓ cups organic flour
(All purpose, whole wheat, multi-grain or any combination)
3 cups organic cane sugar
1 teaspoon sea salt
½ teaspoon baking powder

1 teaspoon baking soda
1½ tablespoons ground Vietnamese cinnamon
1 tablespoon ground nutmeg
1 tablespoon ground cloves

Preheat oven to 350 degrees. Grease muffin pan with non-stick cooking spray, or fill with paper muffin cups and set aside. Mix dry ingredients well, with paddle attachment of electric stand mixer or whisk together in a large bowl, then add:

16 oz. can organic pumpkin puree
4 organic eggs
1 cup extra light olive oil

Stir until combined on low speed of electric or stand mixer, then mix no longer than one minute on medium speed. At this point you can add optional additions and stir until combined. Fill muffin pan cups ¾ full with an ice cream scoop. Sprinkle with course organic raw sugar. Bake 25 minutes or until a toothpick comes out clean. Cool slightly on wire racks, 3-5 minutes, then carefully remove from muffin pan using a smooth bladed knife to loosen the edges. Serve warm with cream cheese or cinnamon butter, or cool completely and store in sealed freezer bags in the freezer. A one-gallon bag will hold 9 muffins. When ready to serve, muffins can be heated directly from the freezer to the microwave for 25-30 seconds. They will taste as if they are fresh from the oven!

optional additions

1 cup chopped walnuts
1 cup fresh cranberries
(or ½ cup of each)

Cinnamon Butter ~
½ cup *(1 stick)* unsalted butter
1 teaspoon Vietnamese cinnamon
Bring butter to room temperature.
Add cinnamon and stir until well combined.

makes 1 dozen

*Or two dozen mini-size muffins

NUTTY BANANA MUFFINS *makes one dozen*

These banana muffins are so moist and flavorful. The batter can also be prepared as banana bread. Serve with mascarpone or cream cheese, honey and toasted walnuts for an extra special treat.

1 cup all purpose flour *(organic)*
½ cup whole wheat flour *(organic)*
1 cup organic cane sugar
½ tablespoon ground Vietnamese cinnamon
1 teaspoon ground nutmeg
1 teaspoon baking soda
¼ teaspoon sea salt

1 teaspoon lemon zest
2 large organic eggs
½ cup extra light olive oil
1 teaspoon Madagascar vanilla extract
2 very ripe bananas, mashed
1 cup walnuts, toasted and chopped
(plus more for serving if desired)

Preheat oven to 350 degrees. Spray muffin pan with non-stick spray or fill with paper muffin cups. Mix dry ingredients well, with electric mixer or paddle attachment of stand mixer, then add eggs, oil, vanilla and bananas. Mix until combined and creamy but no longer than one minute. Stir in 1 cup chopped toasted walnuts. Fill muffin cups ¾ full and bake 22-25 minutes. Cool slightly on wire racks then carefully remove from the muffin pan by running a smooth bladed knife along the edges. Serve warm with cream cheese icing, or cool completely and store in sealed freezer bags in the freezer. A one-gallon bag will hold 9 muffins. When ready to serve, muffins can be heated directly from the freezer to the microwave for 30 seconds (microwave cooking times may vary). They will taste as if they are fresh from the oven! Top with icing and chopped toasted walnuts if desired.

the icing

Simply combine 1 cup mascarpone or cream cheese in a small bowl with 1 tablespoon organic honey. Stir well and spread on muffins.

banana bread

Pour batter into greased or buttered loaf pan, non-stick spray is fine. Bake at 350 degrees for 30 minutes or until a toothpick inserted in the center comes out clean. Cool in pan on rack for 5 minutes, then turn out of pan and continue to cool on rack.

OH HONEY!

VERY BERRY MUFFINS

I like a combination of blueberries, blackberries and raspberries in a fluffy muffin. The flavors of all 3 berries along with a buttery sweet streusel topping, add a bit of zing to this berry muffin.

makes one dozen!

2 cups all purpose flour *(organic)*
1 cup organic cane sugar
½ teaspoon baking powder
½ teaspoon salt
½ teaspoon ground nutmeg
2 tablespoons *cake enhancer**
½ cup organic 2% milk

2 large eggs
6 tablespoons extra light olive oil
½ teaspoon good vanilla extract
  (Madagascar Bourbon Vanilla)
2 cups berries, tossed in 1 tablespoon
  of flour

Preheat oven to 350 degrees. Grease muffin pan with non-stick spray or fill with paper muffin cups. Mix dry ingredients well, then add, milk, eggs, oil and vanilla. Beat with paddle attachment of stand mixer until just blended, no longer than one minute. Gently fold in the berries. With a large ice cream scoop, fill muffin cups 2/3 full and sprinkle with topping, if desired.

Bake 22-25 minutes or until a toothpick inserted in the center of the muffins comes out clean. Let cool in pan 2-3 minutes on wire rack, then remove using a smooth bladed knife to loosen around the edges. Serve warm with butter or cream cheese. Muffins can be kept in the freezer in air tight baggies and reheated in the microwave for 30-35 seconds per muffin straight from the freezer.

the cinnamon streusel

3 tablespoons cold unsalted butter,
  ½ inch cubes
½ cup all purpose flour *(organic)*
3 tablespoons organic raw sugar

1 tablespoon ground cinnamon
Squeeze between fingers to combine
until "crumble" forms.

helpful hints

*Cake Enhancer helps breads, muffins and cakes stay soft and moist. (King Arthur Flour has a very good one). For a gluten-free muffin, substitute all purpose flour with "Cup 4 Cup" gluten-free flour.

EGGS BENEDICTO FOR TWO

There is not a better dish for a special breakfast or brunch than Eggs Benedict. Mine has a rustic Italian flair with a lemony cream sauce instead of traditional hollandaise.

4 large eggs, poached

4 slices rustic Italian bread *(Ciabatta)*, **toasted and buttered** *(1 inch slices)*

4 slices prosciutto

Zest and juice of one lemon

1 tablespoon flat leaf *(Italian)* **parsley, finely chopped**

Lemony cream sauce *(recipe follows)*.

lemony cream sauce

2 tablespoons unsalted butter
2 tablespoons all purpose flour
1 cup milk at room temperature *(2% milk fat)*
1 tablespoon lemon zest
1 tablespoon fresh lemon juice
1 egg yolk
Kosher salt and fresh ground pepper to taste
1 tablespoon flat leaf *(Italian)* **parsley**

silicone egg poaching cup

Melt butter in a small saucepan over medium heat. Sprinkle flour evenly into butter and whisk until smooth. Slowly add milk whisking constantly until well combined. Cook over medium heat continuing to stir. While the sauce is cooking, start your eggs. When the sauce begins to thicken, add lemon zest and salt and pepper to taste. Continue to stir with whisk until sauce is thick and creamy. Remove from heat and quickly whisk egg yolk into sauce. Continue whisking while slowly adding lemon juice. Spoon sauce over eggs immediately and top with flat leaf parsley. Season to taste with salt and pepper if desired.

poached eggs

I like to use silicone egg poaching cups for poaching eggs (pictured above). It makes the process so simple and the eggs turn out perfect every time. Spray egg poaching cups with non-stick spray and carefully fill each with one egg. Fill a medium saucepan or deep sauté pan with 1½ to 2 inches of water and a pinch of kosher salt. Bring water to a simmer over medium to medium-high heat and gently place eggs in their cups into the water. Poach eggs until whites are firm and yolks are still runny, 5-7 minutes. (Or until desired consistency.) To speed the process, loosely cover (tent) with foil and poach for 3-5 minutes.

assembly

Lay two slices of toasted and buttered Ciabatta bread on each of two serving plates. Arrange a slice of prosciutto on each toast. Carefully spoon a poached egg on top of each and finish with lemony cream sauce and fresh chopped parsley. Season to taste with salt and pepper if desired. Serve with a tall cool mimosa or "Gigi Bellini!"

Gigi bellini

Fill a champagne glass or flute with chilled Prosecco. Add a splash of Grand Marnier (orange liqueur) and enjoy!

FRIED EGG CAESAR

serves 4

When I am entertaining house guests for brunch, I like to combine a traditional breakfast dish with a great lunch salad all in the same dish. This is a great brunch salad that is a perfect combination of both. I serve with a light and dry Pinot Grigio, a side of fresh sliced cantaloupe melon and plenty of extra bread sticks for dipping!

Lemony Caesar Salad *(see recipe, page 42)*
4 large eggs, fried to medium *(or to your liking)*
8 slices prosciutto
Course sea salt or kosher salt to taste
Freshly ground pepper to taste
½ cup Parmigiano Reggiano Cheese *(freshly grated)*
1 package Italian Bread Sticks *(such as "Grissini")*

Plate Lemony Caesar Salad on each of 4 serving plates. In the center of each salad lay one slice of prosciutto, folding over to form a bed for one fried egg to rest on top.

Spray a large skillet with non-stick spray and place over medium heat. When the pan is hot, carefully crack eggs, one at a time, into the pan. You can also crack eggs into a glass, one at a time, and pour from the glass into the pan. This simply makes it a little easier to prevent the yolk from breaking. When the edges of the egg are dry and the egg white begins to appear to be cooked through, about 2 minutes, turn heat off and cook 45 seconds more for medium. If you like your eggs a little more well done, allow to sit in the pan until desired temperature is reached. Place one egg on top of each bed of prosciutto and season to taste with course salt and freshly ground pepper. Generously spoon grated cheese around the egg and garnish with a bread stick wrapped in prosciutto.

Serve with extra bread sticks (in a glass or vase) for dipping.

GRUYERE~MUSHROOM OMELETTE

Fluffy, savory and cheesy, this omelette has it all! The secret to a fabulously fluffy omelette is all in the whisk. The more air you bring into the eggs, the fluffier the omelette. I like to serve an omelette with a side of halved grape or cherry tomatoes tossed with extra virgin olive oil and good balsamic vinegar, just enough to coat. Add a little course sea salt and pepper to taste and finish with a few fresh basil leaves.

3 large fresh organic eggs
1 tablespoon water
1 cup sliced mixed mushrooms
  (cremini, shitake, button)
1 tablespoon olive oil
½ teaspoon fresh thyme leaves,
  chopped
½ cup Gruyere cheese, grated

1 teaspoon flat leaf parsley, finely
  chopped
1 teaspoon fresh chives, finely chopped
1 tablespoon Parmigiano Reggiano
  cheese, finely grated
Kosher salt and freshly ground pepper
to taste

Bring a sauté pan with 1 tablespoon olive oil to medium heat and add mushrooms, thyme, a pinch of kosher salt and ground pepper. Sauté, stirring occasionally, until the mushrooms are cooked through and beginning to caramelize. Transfer mushrooms to a bowl and set aside. Spray the same pan with non-stick cooking spray and return to medium heat. Meanwhile, whisk the eggs briskly in a medium bowl with 1 tablespoon of water. When thoroughly combined and foamy, pour into the sauté pan. Allow the eggs to cook almost completely through over medium heat, until the edges are dry and the center is set. Using a spatula, loosen the edges of the omelette, all the way around the pan and flip over completely. Cook for another minute or so, just until cooked through. Loosen the omelette again with your spatula, and flip over completely with the original cooked side down.

Add the mushrooms, chives and Gruyere cheese, just off center, and using your spatula, fold the omelette over in half, covering the filling completely. Turn the heat off and allow to rest while the cheese melts, about a minute. Gently slide the omelette out of the pan onto an individual serving plate. Top with more grated Gruyere cheese, Parmigiano Reggiano, parsley, chives and salt and pepper to taste.

Drizzle with a little extra virgin olive oil and serve immediately.

FLUFFY LEMON PANCAKES

serves 2 to 4

My husband, Jeff, and I spend several weeks each summer in the beautiful Colorado Rockies to escape the heat and humidity in the southeast. One of our first summers there, we celebrated my birthday with breakfast at the Little Nell in Aspen. The Lemon Soufflé Pancakes were incredible, so light and fluffy. I couldn't wait to get home to try to duplicate them. Here is what I came up with. I think I got pretty close!

3/4 cup organic all purpose flour
2 tablespoons organic cane sugar
1 teaspoon baking powder
1/2 teaspoon sea salt (or kosher salt)
3/4 cup milk (2% or non-fat)
1 egg, separated

1 teaspoon Madagascar vanilla extract
1 tablespoon fresh lemon juice; plus 1/8 teaspoon lemon juice
1 tablespoon fresh lemon zest
Berry coulis, maple syrup and fresh berries for serving

Heat a serving plate in the oven at approximately 200 degrees. In a medium bowl, whisk together dry ingredients. In a separate small bowl, whisk milk and egg yolk. Add to flour mixture along with lemon zest, 1 tablespoon lemon juice and vanilla and whisk until thoroughly combined. In a separate bowl, beat egg white until foamy with electric mixer or whisk attachment of stand mixer. Add 1/8 teaspoon lemon juice and continue to beat until stiff but not dry, when soft peaks form.

Gently fold egg whites into the batter. Spray a nonstick pan or griddle with butter flavor non-stick cooking spray (or use a pat of unsalted butter to grease the cooking surface) and heat over medium heat. When the pan is warm, pour 1/4 cup of the batter for each pancake onto the heated surface and cook on both sides until golden brown. Remove to a heated serving plate and repeat until all pancakes are cooked. Place pancakes on individual serving plates and sprinkle with confectioners (powdered) sugar using a small, fine mesh strainer. Just give it a few taps.

Garnish with fresh berries (raspberries, blueberries, or blackberries) and serve with berry coulis and warm maple syrup.

berry coulis

Simply bring 1 cup berries, 1/4 cup water and one tablespoon sugar to a boil. Reduce heat and simmer until the berries have reduced into the water and sugar, stirring occasionally, 10-15 minutes. Place a bowl under a fine mesh strainer and pour coulis through the strainer to remove seeds. Stir to press the coulis through to the bowl with a spoon or spatula.

simple variation

Use your favorite Pancake Mix! (Mine is Maple Grove Farms Buttermilk and Honey)

1 cup Buttermilk Pancake Mix
1/2 cup water
1 egg, separated
1 tablespoon fresh lemon juice

1 tablespoon extra light olive oil
1 tablespoon fresh lemon zest
1/8 teaspoon fresh lemon juice

Mix together the pancake mix, water, oil, 1 tablespoon lemon juice and egg yolk until just combined. Stir in lemon zest and set aside. Beat egg white until foamy and add lemon juice. Continue to beat until stiff, but not dry (soft peaks). Gently fold egg whites into the batter. Follow previous cooking and serving instructions.

It's all about the lunch with these super lunch salads. Fresh and flavorful, perfect for a complete meal, whether it's for lunch or even a light dinner entrée, your palate will be utterly satisfied with every bite. Simple *and* spectacular!

LET'S DO LUNCH

salads!

CAPRESE SALAD

One of the greatest joys of summer is when fresh heirloom tomatoes are in season. They are beautiful, flavorful and available in nearly every color of the rainbow. I love to serve them with fresh Bufala mozzarella in a traditional Caprese salad, "salad of Capri." Bufala mozzarella is made from the milk of water buffalo, which is sweeter and creamier than cow's milk with more calcium and protein, but less cholesterol. It's smooth, springy texture and mild, floral flavor make Bufala mozzarella the "queen" of Italian cheeses. There is quite simply no substitute in a true Caprese salad.

bufala mozzarella

1 ball (8 oz.) fresh Bufala mozzarella, sliced in ½ inch slices

4-5 heirloom tomatoes in various colors and sizes

½ cup fresh basil leaves, julienne (plus a sprig for garnish if desired)

¼ cup very good extra virgin olive oil (first cold pressed)

Course sea salt and freshly ground pepper to taste

Parmigiano Reggiano Cheese, shaved with cheese plane or vegetable peeler

Drain water from the mozzarella and press between paper towels to drain the excess moisture. Slice the cheese and arrange on a serving platter. Slice tomatoes in ¼ inch slices and place on top and around the cheese. Season to taste with salt and pepper. Just before serving, drizzle olive oil over cheese and tomatoes and top with julienne of fresh basil. Finish with shavings of Parmigiano Reggiano cheese.

Serve with a chilled glass of crisp, dry Pinot Grigio and savor every bite!

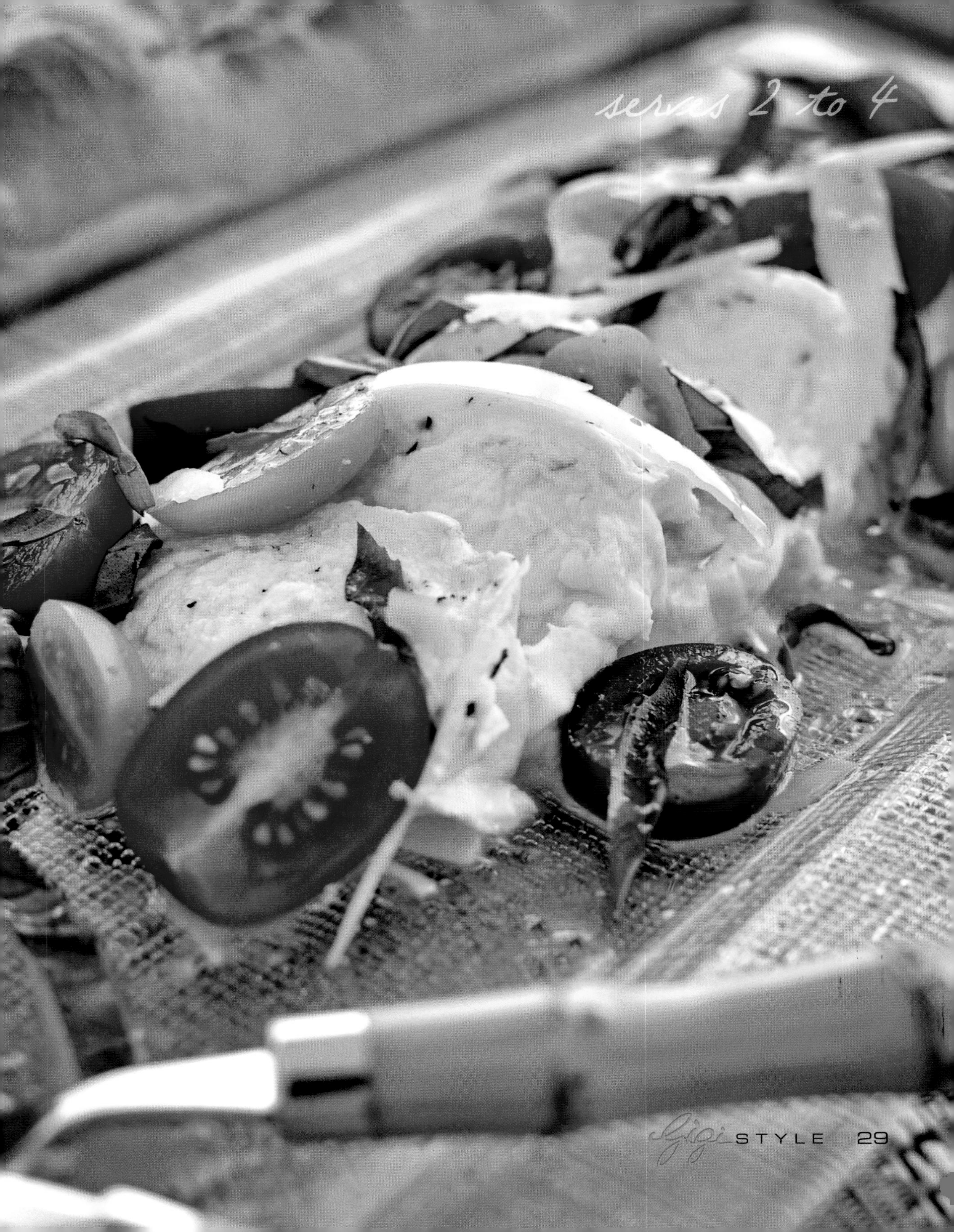
serves 2 to 4

CHICKEN COBB SALAD

A traditional Chicken Cobb Salad with a tangy twist, Dijon-Balsamic dressing. Use my Easy Roast Chicken recipe or a grocery store bought rotisserie chicken, which makes it so simple with very little preparation time. A little carving and chopping and you have a complete meal.

1 whole roasted chicken
(a store bought rotisserie chicken is fine)

2 cups cherry tomatoes, quartered

2 medium Hass avocados, sliced

8 oz. package organic mixed baby greens

6 medium hard boiled eggs, halved or quartered

1 tablespoon freshly chopped chives

½ cup crumbled blue cheese

½ pound crispy Bacon, crumbled *(optional)*

Carve chicken by first removing wings, then leg quarters (legs and thighs) and set aside. Taking your knife along either side of the breast bone, remove each breast half and cut crosswise into 1-inch slices. Combine greens and tomatoes in a medium bowl. Toss with half of the dressing and place onto the center of a serving plate. Arrange chicken breast slices along one side of the bed of greens and avocado slices and eggs on the either side of the vegetables. Drizzle remaining dressing over the chicken and avocado. Finish with fresh chopped chives, kosher salt and fresh ground pepper to taste. Top with crumbled blue cheese and chopped crispy bacon if desired.

dijon-balsamic dressing

¾ cup extra virgin olive oil

2 tablespoons aged balsamic vinegar

1 tablespoon classic Dijon mustard

1 tablespoon dry white wine

½ teaspoon course sea salt or kosher salt

½ teaspoon freshly ground pepper

½ teaspoon Herbs de Provence

Whisk vinegar and mustard together in a small bowl. Stream oil into the dressing, whisking constantly until thoroughly combined. Add salt, pepper, herbs and white wine and whisk until smooth.

serves 4 to 6

FENNEL~ORANGE SALAD

Fennel has such a wonderful anise flavor, and crisp bite, a natural with the citrusy sweetness of orange. I balance this salad with salty kalamata olives and a light dressing. This refreshing and delicate salad is wonderful just as it is, or served alongside fish or chicken.

- 1 medium navel orange, zested, segmented, peel and pith removed
- 1 medium fennel bulb, halved, cored and thinly sliced
- 5 oz. package organic baby spinach leaves
- 7 oz. package organic romaine lettuce leaves
- 1 tablespoon chives, finely chopped
- 1 tablespoon flat leaf parsley, chopped
- Fleur de sel crystals *(course sea salt)* and freshly ground pepper to taste

Zest orange and cut into segments with a pairing knife, removing peel and all white pith. Set aside. Rinse and thoroughly dry spinach and romaine leaves. Cut romaine leaves horizontally into 2-3 inch strips and place in a large bowl with spinach leaves. Toss lightly with just enough of the dressing to coat the leaves. Using salad tongs, place on a chilled serving platter or individual serving plates. Arrange fennel, orange segments and olives on top of the lettuces and drizzle with more of the dressing. Finish with chives, parsley, orange zest, fleur de sel and ground pepper to taste.

the dressing

- ¼ cup fresh lemon juice
- ¾ cup extra virgin olive oil
- 1 tablespoon orange zest
- 1 teaspoon Herbs de Provence
- Pinch fleur de sel crystals *(course sea salt)*
- Freshly ground pepper to taste

In a small bowl, whisk together olive oil and lemon until emulsified. Add remaining ingredients and stir until thoroughly combined.

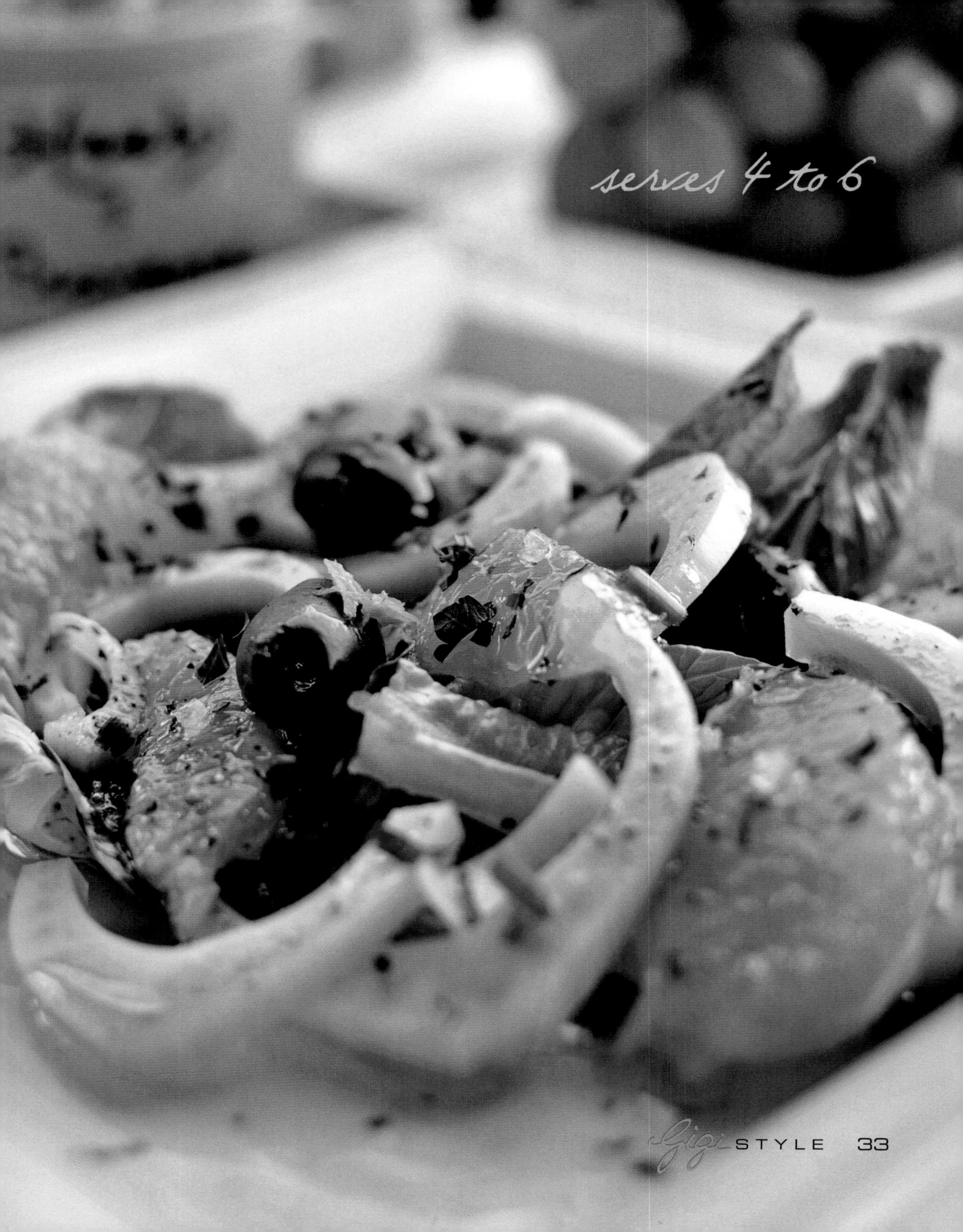

serves 4 to 6

KALE SALAD WITH QUINOA *serves 4 to 6*

The sweetness and combination of flavors and textures in this power green salad is nothing short of heterogeneous. Healthy kale balances the sweet dressing, while chewy dried cranberries and crunchy marcona almonds add layers of texture. The secret is the lemon infused olive oil dressing, this salad has it all.

3 cups kale, thoroughly rinsed, dried and chopped, stems removed

2 cups spinach leaves

1 cup snow peas, blanched

1 cup dried cranberries

1 cup whole marcona almonds

½ cup red quinoa, cooked according to package directions

Course sea salt *(Fleur de sel)* and fresh ground pepper to taste

Blanch snow peas in 3 cups boiling salted water for approximately one minute. Remove with a slotted spoon or spider immediately to an ice bath to cool, then to paper towels to dry. Place rinsed and dried greens in a large salad bowl and toss with ½ of the dressing. Add cooked quinoa and toss again to coat the quinoa with dressing. Add remaining ingredients and lightly toss. Finish with a sprinkling of Fleur de sel (course sea salt). Drizzle with more dressing if desired, and serve.

the dressing

1 cup lemon infused olive oil

1 teaspoon organic honey

1 teaspoon course sea salt

½ teaspoon fresh ground pepper

Carefully zest two lemons with a vegetable peeler into strips, be careful not to take any of the white pith with the lemon peel. Place in a small saucepan with 1 cup extra virgin olive oil. Warm over low heat for 10-15 minutes, infusing the lemon into the oil. Remove from heat and cool to room temperature. With a slotted spoon, remove lemon peel and pour infused oil into a small bowl. Whisk in the honey, salt and pepper.

variation

If you'd like to add a little protein to this power packed salad, top with a simply grilled breast of chicken or grilled salmon filet. Drizzle with remaining dressing and season with course sea salt and freshly ground pepper.

LEMONY CAESAR SALAD

My version of the classic…an olive oil based, anchovy free variety, but not short on garlic or delicious and nutty Aged Parmigiano Reggiano, the champagne of cheese! Jeff likes to finish his with crumbled Gorgonzola cheese, which I serve in a separate bowl along side of the salad.

16 oz. organic romaine lettuce, chilled

1½ cups grated Parmigiano Reggiano cheese

1 cup pitted kalamata olives

Ciabatta croutons *(optional)*

the dressing

¾ cup very good extra virgin olive oil *(first cold pressed)*

¼ cup fresh squeezed lemon juice

1 teaspoon grated lemon zest

1-2 garlic cloves *(thinly sliced)*

½ teaspoon course sea salt *(or kosher salt)*

½ teaspoon freshly ground black pepper

Place olive oil in small bowl. Thinly slice garlic cloves and add to oil. Allow to rest and fuse into the oil for 3-4 hours. Remove garlic from oil with a small slotted spoon. Whisk in lemon juice until well combined. The dressing will have a bright yellow hue. Add lemon zest, salt and pepper, and whisk thoroughly to combine. Meanwhile, slice ciabatta bread into 1-inch cubes. Drizzle with olive oil and course salt, and toast on a sheet pan under the broiler until browned and crispy.

assembly

Cut lettuce crosswise into relatively bite size pieces and place in a large wooden salad bowl. Add half of the dressing and toss to coat. Add 1 cup of the Parmigiano Reggiano and toss well. If you like more dressing, add now. Gently spoon onto a chilled serving dish or chilled individual salad plates and top with remaining ½ cup of Parmigiano. Finish with more freshly ground pepper to taste and shavings of Parmigiano Reggiano, using a thin cheese plane or vegetable peeler. I like a bowl of kalamata olives on the side, and, of course, Jeff's crumbled Gorgonzola.

variation

For a little added protein, top with a grilled tuna steak, a simply grilled chicken breast or grilled salmon filet.

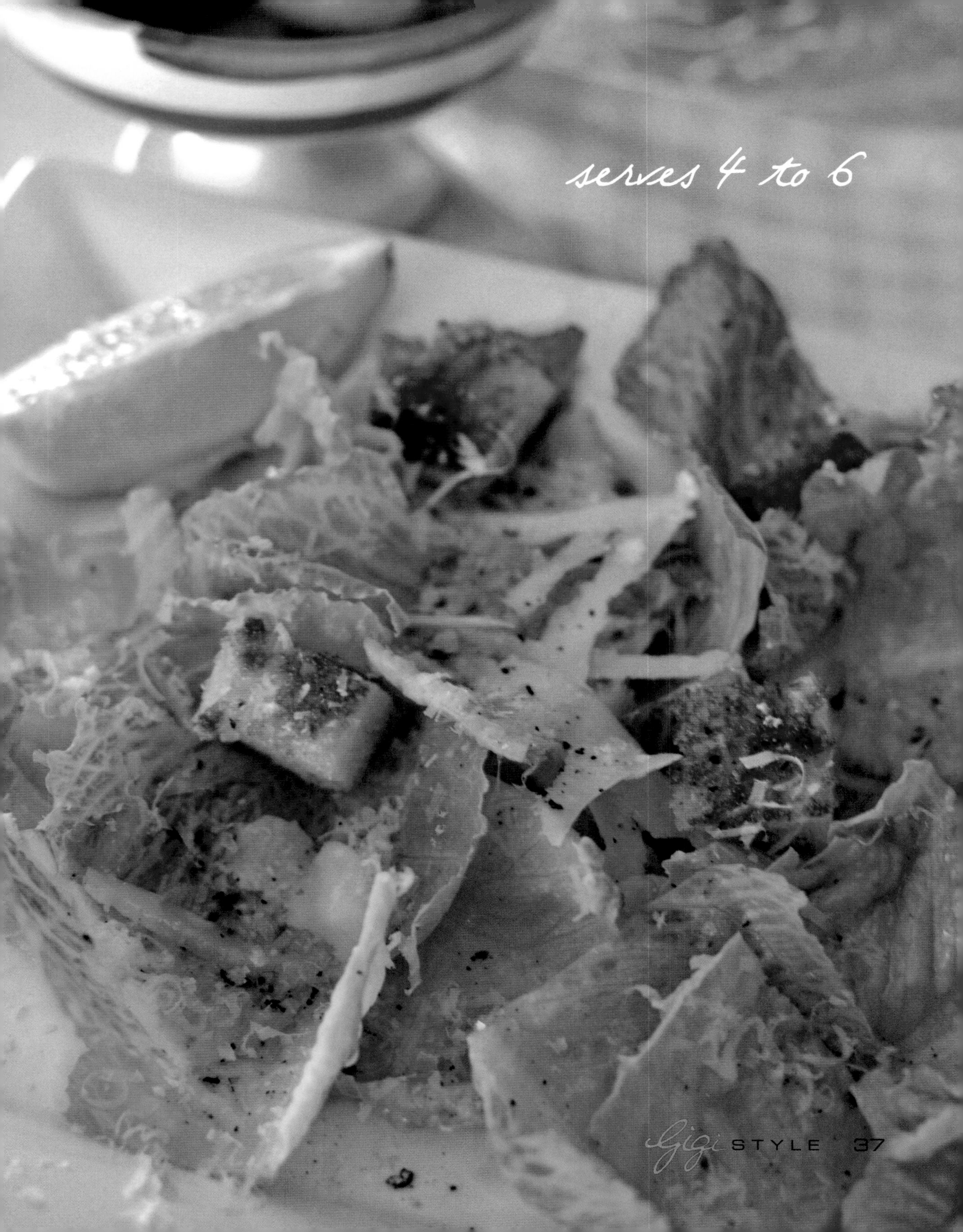
serves 4 to 6

LOBSTER CAESAR

Living in Nassau, Bahamas for several months per year, we eat an abundance of delicious fresh spiny lobster, indigenous to the Bahamas and the country's largest food export. Spiny lobsters have no claws, the best meat is in the tail. I find spiny lobster tail a little more tender and sweeter than a Maine lobster. You will find many great lobster recipes in my book. I love to serve a Lobster Caesar to first time lunch guests to our home. It is light, lemony and delicious, especially with a nice cool glass of Prosecco or Champagne!

Lemony Caesar Salad — reserve ¼ cup dressing *(see recipe)*
Lemon wedges for serving
3-4 broiled or grilled lobster tails

I like my lobster tail a little crispy on the outside, tender and juicy on the inside. Preheat broiler to 500 degrees or grill to high heat. Using kitchen shears, cut the shell of the lobster down the middle to the fan tail. Turn over and cut the ribs of the tail. Holding with the shell side on top, crack the shell apart, carefully, to keep the meat of the tail in tact. Rinse and remove center vein and dry thoroughly on paper towels. Place lobster tails on a sheet pan and drizzle with extra virgin olive oil. Season with course sea salt and freshly ground black pepper. Place under the broiler approximately 6 inches from heat or directly on the grill, until lobster tails begin to brown on the edges and the center appears opaque, 5-7 minutes. Turn the heat off and close the oven door or grill lid to allow the tails to cook through, no more than 5 minutes longer. Be careful not to overcook! Remove from the oven and cool to room temperature.

assembly

Individual Plated Servings
Cut each tail in half lengthwise and set one-half aside for each plate. Cut remaining lobster into 1-2 inch bite size chunks. Toss into the salad and plate onto individual serving plates or bowls. Lay one of the reserved ½ tails on top of each salad and spoon the reserved dressing on each tail. Finish with freshly grated Parmigiano Reggiano cheese and freshly ground black pepper on each salad. Garnish with lemon wedges.

Large Serving Dish
Prepare as above and spoon onto the serving dish. Arrange reserved half tails on top of salad. Finish with grated Parmigiano Reggiano, freshly ground black pepper and a drizzle of reserved dressing over top. Garnish with lemon wedges and serve.

PANZANELLA SALAD

serves 4 to 6

There is no better use for day-old Ciabatta bread or my Rustic Italian Loaf than to prepare a Panzanella Salad. It is fresh and colorful and the chunks of rustic Italian bread make it hearty enough for a lunch on its own, or as a side salad with dinner.

7 oz. package mixed baby greens

7 oz. package romaine lettuce, chopped bite size

1 medium hot house cucumber, cut into ¼ inch slices, then quartered

1 large Hass avocado, cut into large cubes

1 pint small heirloom tomatoes, halved

1 medium shallot, thinly sliced

1 cup whole pitted Kalamata olives

1 each yellow/orange/red bell pepper, cut into strips

4-6 slices day old rustic bread, cut or torn into 1-2 inch cubes

Place lettuces, cucumber, tomatoes, shallot, olives, peppers and bread cubes in a wooden salad bowl. Toss with one cup vinaigrette. Halve avocado lengthwise and separate. Remove pit and cut both sides into large cubes, while still in skin, spoon chunks from each half onto the salad and discard shell. Drizzle with remaining dressing and sprinkle with dried oregano.

vinaigrette dressing

1 cup extra virgin olive oil

⅓ cup fresh lemon juice

1 tablespoon red wine vinegar

1 teaspoon dried oregano

1 teaspoon sea salt or kosher salt

½ teaspoon freshly ground pepper

In a small bowl whisk together extra virgin olive oil and fresh lemon juice until emulsified. Add red wine vinegar, dried oregano, sea salt and freshly ground pepper. Whisk until well combined.

SALMON~SPINACH SALAD

serves 2 to 4

Omega-rich salmon and vitamin-rich spinach, a power packed combo. With asparagus, strawberries and crunchy toasted almonds, this salad is a complete and healthy meal.

2-4 salmon filets

6 oz. package baby spinach leaves

1 cup strawberries, cleaned, hulled and sliced

½ cup whole almonds, toasted

4-6 stalks asparagus, blanched

1 cup pecorino Romano cheese, shredded

Kosher salt and fresh ground pepper to taste

Brush salmon with olive oil and season with course salt and freshly ground pepper. Spray grill pan (or sauté pan) with non-stick spray and heat over medium high heat until hot. Place the salmon flesh side down in the pan and cook until it is nicely browned. Turn over to skin side down and reduce heat to medium low. Cover loosely with foil and allow the fish to steam through, 5-7 minutes for medium rare, 8-10 minutes for medium. To broil the fish simply place salmon skin side down on a broiler pan. Brush with olive oil and season with salt and pepper. Broil on high until the fish is nicely browned, turn the heat off and close the oven door until the fish is cooked through, approximately 5 minutes for medium rare, 8 minutes for medium.

After the salmon has cooked to desired temperature, you can easily remove the skin by taking your knife along the edge of the fish and between the flesh and skin. Loosen the skin with your knife and use a spatula to easily remove the flesh of the salmon to a board. Cut fish into large, but bite size pieces. Meanwhile, blanch asparagus by trimming ends and placing in a sauté pan of boiling water with a pinch of kosher salt. Boil until tender, 2-4 minutes depending on thickness. Remove with tongs directly to a bowl of ice water to stop the cooking, allowing the asparagus to retain its beautiful deep green color. After about a minute, remove to paper towels to dry and cut into 2-inch pieces. Toss spinach, strawberries and asparagus lightly with dressing and season with salt and pepper. Plate vegetables on individual serving plates and top with salmon. Drizzle the salmon with the remaining dressing and top the salad with pecorino and toasted almonds.

dressing

¾ cup extra virgin olive oil
¼ cup white wine vinegar
1 teaspoon organic honey

1 teaspoon fresh lemon juice
¼ teaspoon Worcestershire sauce

In a small bowl whisk together olive oil and vinegar until emulsified. Add honey and lemon and whisk until well combined. Season with salt and pepper to taste.

SOUTHERN WEDGE SALAD

Jeff is not fond of vegetables or salads, but this is one he will eat every day of the week. The crisp combination of romaine and iceberg lettuces, sweet cherry tomatoes and tangy blue cheese make this salad one that everyone will love!

1 large head iceberg lettuce, quartered into wedges *(core removed)*

1 large head romaine lettuce, core removed

4 oz. pickled shallots *(recipe to follow)*

1 pint sweet cherry tomatoes, halved

1 tablespoon flat leaf parsley

½ to 1 cup blue cheese, crumbled

¼ - ½ cup crispy bacon, finely chopped

Remove core from romaine and rinse leaves well. Dry with paper towels and lay 4 leaves on chilled individual serving plates from center to corners. Core iceberg and cut in half. Lay each half with the flat side down, and cut into wedges, either 3 or 4 wedges per half (total of 6 or 8 wedges). Arrange wedges on top of romaine leaves from center to corners. Spoon tomatoes over and around wedges. Place a handful of shallots in the center of the salad and spoon the dressing over each wedge. Top with a sprinkle of the parsley, blue cheese crumbles and chopped bacon.

the shallots

4 oz. shallots, peeled and thinly sliced

½ cup red wine vinegar

¼ cup organic cane sugar

1 teaspoon salt

In a small non-reactive saucepan, dissolve sugar and salt in vinegar over medium high heat. Add shallots and stir. Remove from heat and allow to cool. Drain shallots by pouring the liquid through a fine mess strainer. Set aside. If making in advance, cover and chill until ready to serve.

creamy blue cheese dressing

¼ cup mayonnaise *(light, regular, miracle whip, whatever you prefer)*

¼ cup plain Greek yogurt or sour cream

½ cup buttermilk

1 tablespoon fresh lemon juice

1 teaspoon flat leaf parsley, finely chopped

½ cup blue cheese, crumbled *(Roquefort or Gorgonzola)*

Kosher salt and freshly ground pepper to taste

In a medium bowl, whisk together mayo, yogurt and buttermilk. Add lemon, parsley, salt and pepper and whisk until well combined. Stir in crumbled blue cheese and pour over salad.

blue cheese vinaigrette

— A healthier version than the creamy variety, but not lacking in flavor.

¾ cup extra virgin olive oil

¼ cup fresh lemon juice

1 teaspoon flat leaf parsley,
finely chopped

1 tablespoon Dijon mustard

½ cup blue cheese
(Roquefort or Gorgonzola)

Kosher salt and freshly ground pepper to taste.

Whisk together olive oil, lemon and Dijon until well combined and emulsified. Add parsley, salt and pepper and whisk until combined. Stir in blue cheese crumbles and pour over salad.

TUNA NICOISE SALAD

When I think of summer, I think chilled Rosé wine and Tuna Nicoise Salad. Mine is a little different, made with grilled Ahi tuna instead of the conventional canned tuna, for a more modern and fresh take on the traditional French classic. I serve this light, colorful and flavorful dish on its own for lunch or dinner, just tor the two at us, or for a crowd. Enjoy with a chilled glass of your favorite Rosé wine. I recommend a Rosé from the Provence region of France. It is crisp, dry, light in color and in taste. Delicieux!

the salad

2 large fresh Ahi tuna filets
½ lb. fresh haricot verts
   (French-cut green beans)
½ lb. white of red new potatoes
1 cup grape or cherry tomatoes, halved

2-4 medium hard-boiled eggs, halved
1-2 medium Hass avocados, sliced
8 oz. package spring mix lettuce
½ cup Nicoise olives

Prepare an ice bath with cold water and ice cubes in a medium bowl. Bring I quart of water and I teaspoon kosher salt to a boil. Add green beans and boil until bright green and tender, but still firm, 3-5 minutes. Test with fork or taste. Using tongs or spider, move beans into ice bath to stop cooking. This will also help them to retain their beautiful bright green color. When the beans have cooled, transfer to paper towels and dry completely. Boil potatoes in salted water until tender but still firm, 8-10 minutes. Remove from water with strainer to small bowl and spoon some of the dressing over them while still hot.

When the potatoes have cooled enough to touch, slice in half and stir to coat with the dressing. Brush tuna filets with extra virgin olive oil and season with course salt, pepper and dried oregano flakes. Sear on both sides on grill or grill pan over medium high heat, 1½ to 2 minutes per side. Remove to platter and allow to rest while assembling the salad. Lightly toss mixed greens in ½ cup dressing and place on a serving platter or individual salad plates. Place tuna filets on top of greens and arrange beans, potatoes, tomatoes, eggs and avocado around tuna. Drizzle with remaining dressing and enjoy with a chilled glass of your favorite Rosé.

the dressing

¾ cup extra virgin olive oil
¼ cup fresh lemon juice
1 teaspoon fresh lemon zest
1 tablespoon Dijon mustard
1 tablespoon dry white wine
   (Pinot Grigio)

1 teaspoon fresh thyme leaves, rough chop
1 teaspoon dried oregano
1 teaspoon course sea salt or kosher salt
½ teaspoon course ground pepper

Whisk lemon juice, zest, dijon and white wine together in a small bowl. thyme, oregano, salt and pepper. Slowly stream olive oil into dressing whisking constantly until ingredients are thoroughly combined and emulsified. At this point, the dressing will have a bright yellow hue. Season to taste with more salt and pepper if desired.

A great dressing for any salad, the tangy lemon and dijon are balanced by the acidity of the white wine which also keeps it from separating. Using a really good extra virgin olive oil completes this well rounded and delicious dressing.

BUFALA COURGETTE SALAD

This mozzarella and tomato salad incorporates thinly sliced zucchini (Courgette) and Kalamata olives for a fresh twist on an old favorite. Bufala, made from pasteurized milk from the water buffalo, is the best mozzarella, more flavorful and sweeter than the cows' milk version, but if you can't find bufula, any fresh mozzarella will do. The secret to making this dish "WOW" is in the olive oil. Use a very good, rich and fruity extra virgin oil. It is worth the splurge!

8 ounce ball fresh Bufala mozzarella

1 medium zucchini, very thinly sliced *(ribbons)*

2 cups sweet grape or cherry tomatoes, halved

1 cup whole pitted Kalamata olives

1 cup fresh basil, julienne

1 teaspoon dried oregano

½ cup very good extra virgin olive oil (first cold pressed)

Pinch course sea salt (or Kosher salt)

Freshly ground pepper

Cut cheese into 1-inch slices and arrange on a chilled serving dish or individual salad plates. Cut top and bottom off of zucchini and slice long ways into very thin ribbon-like slices using a mandolin. Arrange by folding over like ribbons over the Bufala slices. Halve tomatoes and scatter around the plate along with olives. Generously drizzle with very good extra virgin olive oil and sprinkle with oregano. Finish with course salt and pepper.

serves 2 to 4

FESTIVE GOAT CHEESE SALAD

The combination of flavors in this colorful salad make it as beautiful as it is delicious! The nuts add a bit of protein and a great crunch, the fruit, a chewy bite of sweetness and the prosciutto on the goat cheese purses, makes the perfect salty finish.

1 large seedless orange
½ cup dried cranberries
1 medium shallot, thinly sliced into small rings
½ cup halved pecans
6 oz. organic spring mixed greens
½ cup extra virgin olive oil
1 teaspoon fresh orange zest

1 tablespoon country-style Dijon mustard
1 tablespoon dry white wine
1 teaspoon dried herbs for flavor (*i.e. oregano, marjoram, etc.*)
Course sea salt and freshly ground pepper to taste
6-8 goat cheese purses (*1 per serving*)

Prepare goat cheese purses (recipe below). While they are browning, place mixed greens in a large wooden salad bowl. Zest the orange with a good zester (my favorite is Microplane) and set zest aside. Peel the rest of the white pith from orange and slice into segments, removing any other white pith from the center. Add to the salad bowl along with the shallot, cranberries and nuts.

In a small bowl, whisk together olive oil, Dijon, orange zest and white wine until smooth. Add dried herbs, salt and pepper and whisk until combined. Gently toss dressing into salad. At this point you can either place the goat cheese purses on top of the salad in the serving bowl for serving, or plate on individual salad plates, finishing each individual serving with one goat cheese purse.

goat cheese purses

1 goat cheese log (*chevre*), hardened in freezer

6-8 slices prosciutto

Cut goat cheese into ½ inch slices and flatten into rounds. By chilling first in the freezer, the cheese is much easier to slice. Wrap each round in one-half slice of prosciutto making sure to cover all of the cheese with the prosciutto and seal tightly using your fingers. Spray a small sauté pan generously with non-stick spray (I like organic olive oil spray) and bring to medium high heat. Quickly sear each purse until the prosciutto is just browned, turn and brown the other side. Set purses aside until you are ready to assemble the salad.

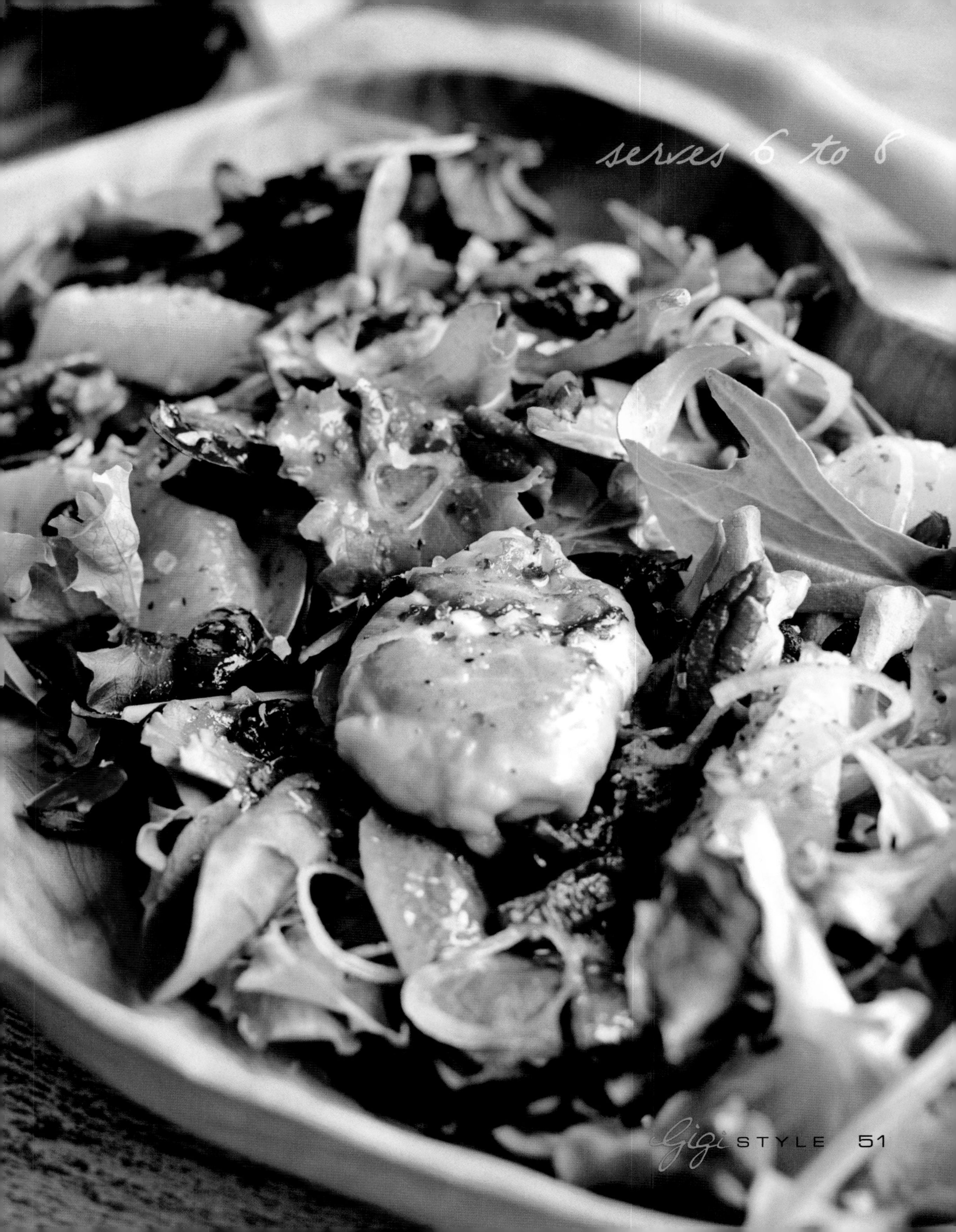
serves 6 to 8

Appetizers SOUPS
& SMALL PLATES

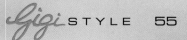

BRIE EN CROUTE

My *go-to* appetizer. It can be prepared so many different ways, so incredibly simply and with very little prep time. Rich, warm, gooey and sweet, this one is always a crowd pleaser. I like to choose seasonal ingredients for the filling and garnishes or flavors that compliment the menu (a few variations listed below). Serve with water crackers and thinly sliced toasted baguette.

1 sheet frozen Puff Pastry dough
(such as Pepperidge farm)

8 ounce round French Brie or
Camembert Cheese

1 tablespoon fruit preserves

¼ cup toasted sliced almonds

1 medium egg, whisked for egg wash

Drizzle of organic honey

Preheat oven to 400 degrees. On a lightly floured surface, roll pastry to ⅛ inch thickness. Carefully cut the Brie in half horizontally to make two equal disks. Set top half aside. Spread preserves starting in the center of the bottom half leaving approximately ¼ inch border around the edges. Replace the top half of the Brie and place the Brie "sandwich" on top of the pastry. Fold edges of the pastry over the Brie and seal tightly, smoothing the edges. Remove any excess pastry with a paring knife. Using the same knife, make slits in the top of the pastry to allow the steam from inside to escape while baking. Place the Brie in pastry on a foil lined baking sheet. Lightly whisk the egg with a fork and using a pastry brush, evenly brush egg wash on top and all sides of the pastry. Bake until beautifully browned, about 15 minutes. Allow the Brie to rest for at least 10-15 minutes after removing from the oven for the cheese to set before cutting into it. I like to top with toasted sliced almonds and a drizzle of organic honey.

variations

Blackberry or strawberry preserves for the filling with fresh berries to accompany the brie on the serving platter. Fig preserves for the filling with fresh black mission figs, halved (when in season) or dried figs. Ginger preserves for the filling with sliced apples and pears (tossed in fresh lemon juice to keep them from turning brown). Be creative with your own favorite combinations!

Fun Decorative Additions: You may like to roll the excess pastry dough to ⅛ inch thickness and cut with a small decorative cookie cutter. I have a little heart shaped cutter for Valentine's Day, in the fall I use a maple leaf cutter, at Thanksgiving a pumpkin shape and at Christmas I use a little Christmas tree. Simply cut as many decorative patterns as you want and place them on the brie after you have applied the egg wash, which will act as glue for your decoration. Brush with a little more egg wash and bake as directed.

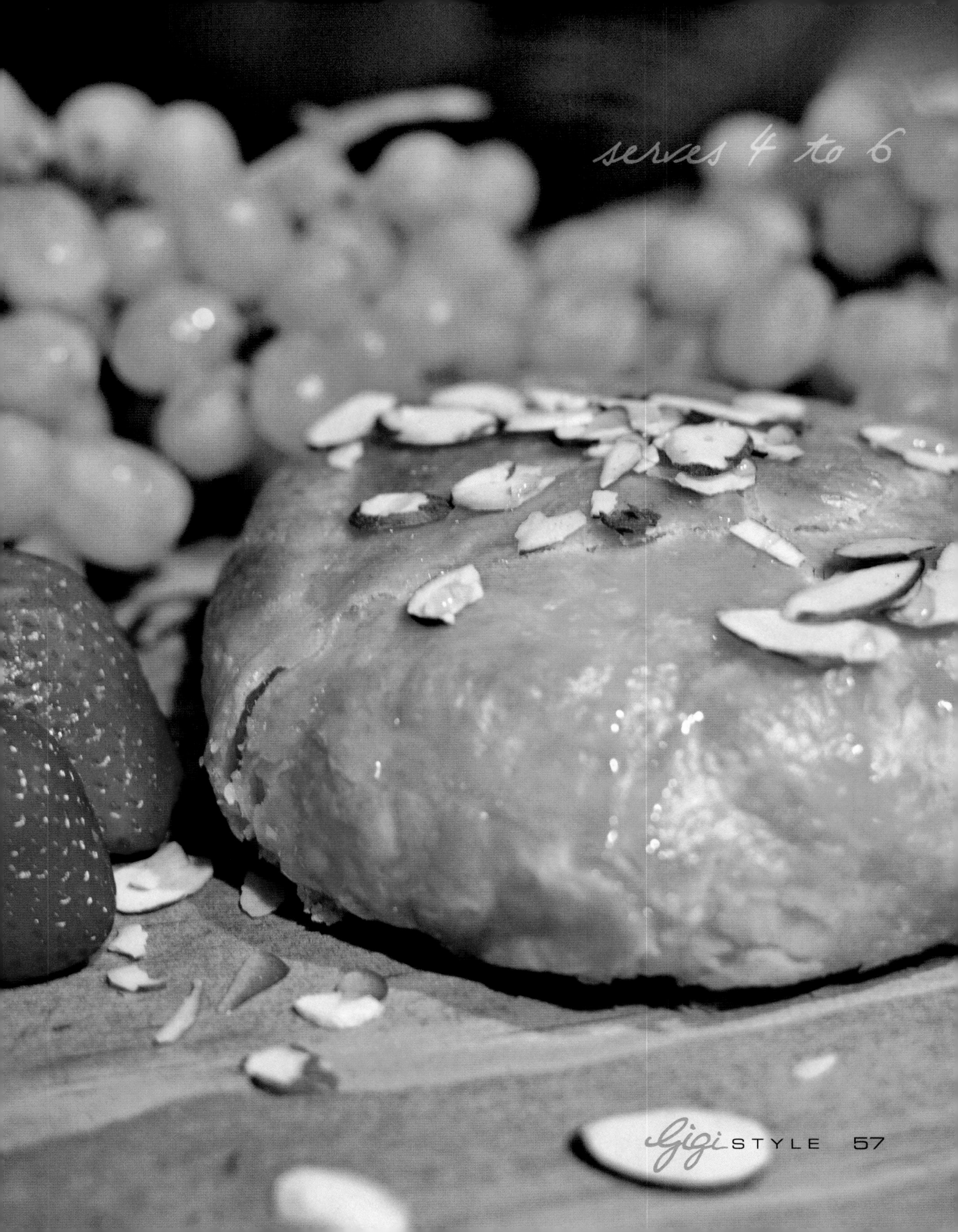
serves 4 to 6

FUNGHI BRIE APPETIZER

serves 4 to 6

Using my Simple Sautéed Mushrooms recipe for the mushrooms, a wheel of soft ripe cheese and toasted baguette slices, this warm and creamy appetizer tantalizes the senses. Serve with your favorite glass of wine for a bit of savory decadence to your wine and cheese.

6-inch wheel of soft ripened cheese, Brie or Camembert

1 recipe Simple Sauté Mushrooms (*Accompaniments & Tasteful Sides*)

1 French baguette

Fresh chives, finely chopped, plus a few whole sprigs for garnish

Fresh thyme sprigs

Course salt and fresh ground pepper to taste

Preheat oven to 400 degrees. Slice baguette into ½ inch slices, drizzle with olive oil and sprinkle with course sea salt, ground pepper and dried oregano. Toast in the oven on a sheet pan until browned and crispy, 15 minutes. With a sharp flat bladed knife, carefully cut the top rind off of the cheese and place back inside its wooden crate. Place on top of a sheet of heavy-duty aluminum foil leaving a 3-inch border. Spoon mushrooms in the center of the Brie and crimp the foil around the edges of the wooden crate to protect from burning. Place on sheet pan and into the oven until the cheese begins to soften and brown slightly, 10-15 minutes. Remove from the oven and allow to set for 5-10 minutes. Remove foil and place Brie in its crate on serving platter. Season with more fresh thyme leaves, course sea salt, fresh ground pepper and freshly chopped chives. Garnish with sprigs of thyme and chives. Serve with toasted baguette slices.

GIGI'S GUACAMOLE

Fresh and flavorful, this tangy guacamole makes a healthy munchie or compliment to salads and tacos. Add a perfect margarita, nothing short of a fabulous fiesta on the palate!

4-6 large Hass avocados
1 medium shallot, finely chopped
4 garlic cloves, minced
1 fresh lime, juiced
1 tablespoon lime zest
1 fresh lemon, juiced

1 tablespoon lemon zest
1 tablespoon fresh orange zest
1 teaspoon dried oregano
1 tablespoon fresh cilantro or flat leaf parsley, finely chopped
Course sea salt and fresh ground pepper to taste

Halve avocados, remove pit and scoop meat with a spoon into a large wooden salad bowl. Add the juices and zest of the lemon and lime and mash the avocado and juice together with a fork. At this point you can mash just until chunky "salsa" style, or until smooth and creamy if you prefer a more pureed style guacamole, but leave some of the pieces of avocado in tact.

Combine with remaining ingredients, gently stirring with a spatula to combine. Serve with your favorite chips or vegetables for dipping. Don't forget the perfect margarita!

serves 8 to 10

LOBSTER WONTONS

serves 6 to 10

This light appetizer is cool and refreshing! I love to serve with champagne or Prosecco as a welcome starter for a summer dinner party. The wonton and celery give a crunchy bite and the tanginess of the lime sparks the senses. But the real secret is the Meyer Lemon, a hybrid cross between a lemon and mandarin orange. Meyer lemons are aromatic, floral and surprisingly sweet.

the wontons

1 package of 30 wontons

Preheat oven to 350 degrees. Place one wonton in each cup of a mini-muffin pan, pressing the dough down into the sides of the cup leaving the pointed edges up to form a basket. Bake for 10 minutes or until lightly brown and crispy. Remove from oven and allow to cool in muffin pan on wire rack for a few minutes. Carefully remove each wonton basket.

the filling

1 Broiled Lobster Tail (8 oz. see recipe)

1 tablespoon shallot, finely minced

1 tablespoon fresh mint, finely chopped

2 tablespoons cilantro, finely chopped

¼ cup celery, ¼ inch dice

¼ cup hothouse cucumber, ¼ inch dice

¼ cup mango, ¼ inch dice

1 tablespoon extra virgin olive oil

1 tablespoon fresh lime juice

1 tablespoon lime zest (approximately 1 lime)

1 tablespoon fresh Meyer lemon zest (from 1 lemon)

1 tablespoon fresh Meyer lemon juice

1 teaspoon course sea salt or Kosher salt

¼ teaspoon freshly ground pepper

¼ teaspoon cumin

Crème Fraiche (optional)

Prepare lobster and allow it to cool, cut into ½ inch pieces and place in a medium bowl with shallot, mint, cilantro, celery, cucumber and mango. In a separate small bowl whisk together olive oil, lime and Meyer lemon zest and juice. Add cumin, salt and pepper and whisk thoroughly. Add to the lobster mixture and stir well to combine. Refrigerate for 1 hour. Place a spoonful of the lobster filling into each wonton and serve. For a hint of decadence, top with a small dollop of crème fraiche (or sour cream) and sprinkle with finely chopped chives.

BAHAMIAN CONCH
~OR CLAM~ CHOWDER

Perhaps my favorite seafood chowder anywhere, is the conch chowder of the Bahamas. Aromatic and spicy, with sweet Johnnycake for dipping, this thick chowder warms the senses.

2 stalks celery, finely chopped

1 large yellow onion, finely chopped

2 medium carrots, finely chopped

1 pound fresh conch or steamed clams, chopped

3 cups water

½ cup tomato paste

2 large bay leaves

1 tablespoon fresh thyme leaves, chopped

1 teaspoon dried oregano leaves

3 tablespoons extra virgin olive oil

½ teaspoon crushed red pepper, or to taste

¼ cup flat leaf parsley, chopped

Kosher salt and ground pepper to taste

Make a roux by whisking 1 tablespoon flour into ½ cup of water in a small bowl. Set aside. Heat oil over medium heat in a stock pot and add vegetables. Saute' until tender, 5-7 minutes. Stir in tomato paste until evenly blended. Add conch (or clams) and simmer 2-3 minutes. Add water, thyme, bay leaves, oregano, salt, pepper and red pepper. Stir together and slowly add roux, stirring constantly until well blended and chowder has thickened somewhat, 15-20 minutes while simmering. Do not boil.

Remove from heat and allow flavors to meld, 30-45 minutes. Re-heat slowly over medium heat and ladle into individual serving bowls. Sprinkle with fresh flat leaf parsley and serve with Johnnycake.

the johnnycake

2 large eggs

1 cup milk, 2% milk-fat

¼ cup light molasses

1 tablespoon extra light olive oil

1¼ cup all purpose flour

¾ cup fine cornmeal

¼ cup organic cane sugar

1½ teaspoons baking powder

1 teaspoon course sea salt or kosher salt

Preheat oven to 325 degrees. Spray two loaf pans with non-stick spray. Whisk dry ingredients together, then add eggs, milk, molasses and olive oil. Divide batter and bake 40-45 minutes until golden brown and toothpick inserted in center comes out clean. Cool in pans on wire racks for 10 minutes, then turn out of pan and continue to cool. Cut into one inch slices. Johnnycake also makes a fantastic shortcake for berries and/or peaches!

EASY TOMATO SOUP

The easiest homemade tomato soup you will ever prepare, and it is fabulous. Fresh and fragrant, warm and soothing. The best rainy day comfort soup in the world. With a Ciabatta crouton and lots of love, this soup makes everyone feel good!

28 oz. can San Marzano diced
  tomatoes

1 garlic clove, minced

¼ cup extra virgin olive oil, plus
  a drizzle to finish

1 tablespoon red wine vinegar
  (or dry red wine)

1 teaspoon dried oregano

¼ cup fresh chives, chopped

¼ cup Parmigiano Reggiano cheese,
  finely grated

Kosher salt and ground pepper
to taste

Place tomatoes, garlic, ¼ cup olive oil, oregano, red wine vinegar, salt and pepper in a (Vitamix) blender or food processor. Blend on high until smooth and creamy, 30 seconds to 1 minute. Pour into a medium saucepan and heat over medium low heat until tepid.
Pour into individual serving bowls and dress with a toasted
Ciabatta crouton. Sprinkle with Parmigiano
Reggiano cheese and chives.
Drizzle with a rich and fruity extra
virgin olive oil and season to taste
with course ground black pepper.

serves 2 to 4

HEARTY KALE MINESTRONE

A healthy, modern twist on this classic Italian vegetable soup. It is as colorful as it is flavorful and stock piled with nutrients. I use red quinoa instead of the conventional pasta and replace white beans with garbanzos (chick peas) for a firmer texture. Fresh autumn harvest vegetables and kale make this simple and healthy soup perfect when there is a chill in the air.

¼ cup extra virgin olive oil

1 medium yellow onion, chopped

2 carrots, sliced in ¼ inch rounds

1 stalk celery, diced

1 teaspoon dried oregano

2 cloves garlic, minced

½ teaspoon red pepper flakes

2 medium zucchini, 1-inch dice

1 medium yellow squash, 1-inch dice

2 cups French green beans, 1-inch chop

4 cups water

2 cups crushed tomatoes (canned San Marzano)

1 cup garbanzo beans, strained and thoroughly rinsed

½ cup red quinoa

1 cup kale leaves, chopped horizontally into 1-inch strips

1 teaspoon each kosher salt and fresh ground pepper, or to taste

1-2 avocados, sliced

½ cup Parmigiano Reggiano cheese, freshly grated

¼ cup flat leaf parsley, finely chopped

Place olive oil in a 3 quart dutch oven or stock pot (I like to use my Le Creuset 3-quart oval dutch oven) and heat over medium heat. Add onion, carrot, celery and oregano and cook 3-5 minutes until the vegetables begin to soften. Stir in garlic and red pepper and cook no longer than 1 minute. Add zucchini, squash, green beans and stir to combine. Pour in tomatoes and water and season with kosher salt and pepper. Bring to a boil. Reduce heat to medium low and simmer soup for 20-30 minutes, stirring occasionally. Add garbanzos and quinoa and cover until quinoa is cooked, 10-15 minutes. Remove cover and stir in kale, simmer 3-5 minutes longer, until kale is tender, but still vibrantly green. Ladle soup into individual serving bowls and top each with a few slices of avocado. Finish with grated Parmigiano Reggiano cheese, flat leaf parsley for a dash of fresh, and a drizzle of extra virgin olive oil.

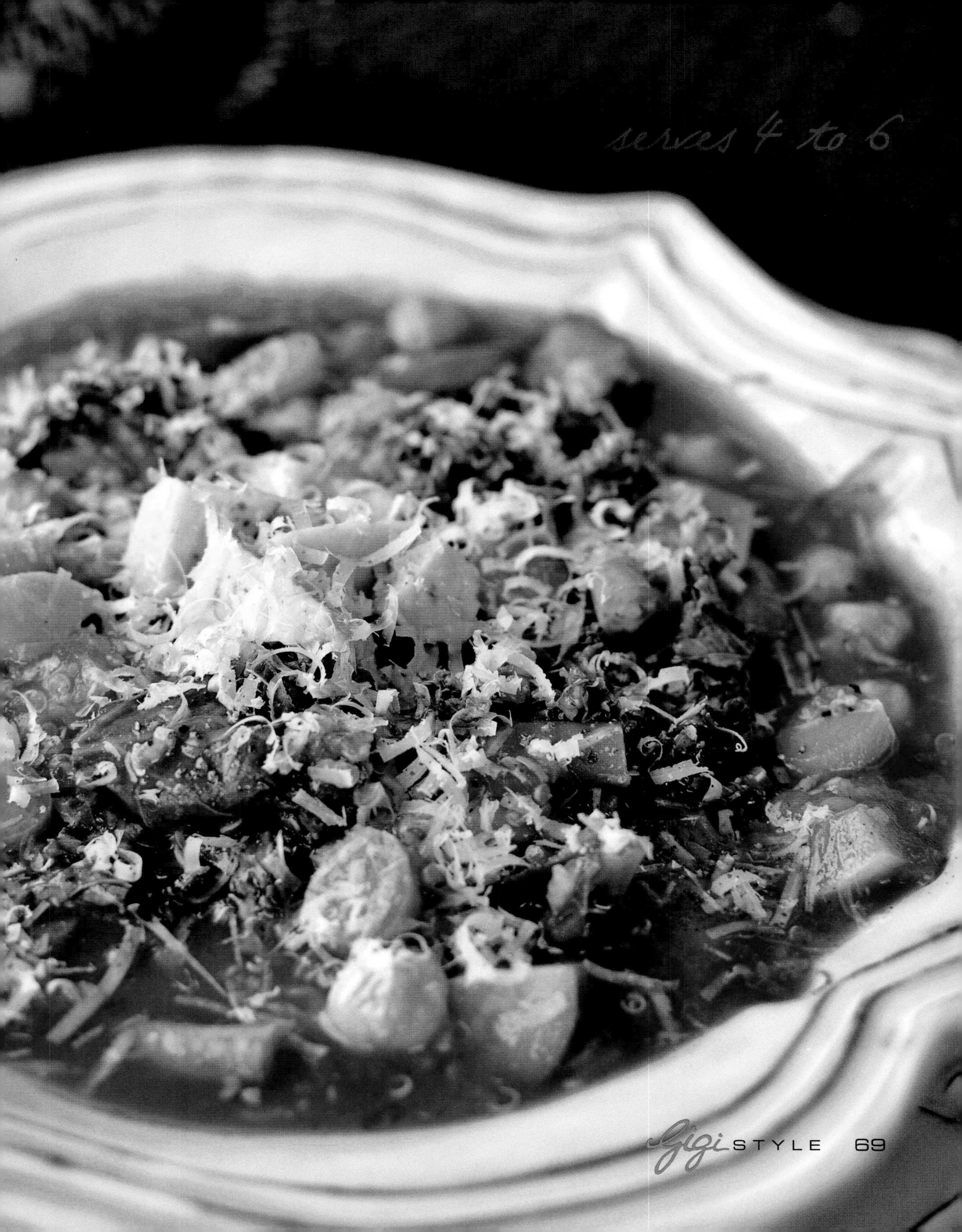
serves 4 to 6

LOW COUNTRY SHRIMP BOIL

serves 6 to 8

A South Carolina Low Country Institution. The shrimp from these coastal waters is quite possibly the sweetest, most delicious shrimp anywhere. Traditionally served on newspaper for easy clean up, this dish is so simple to prepare for a crowd.

2-3 pounds large shrimp, 15-20 count
1 pound kielbasa sausage,1 inch slices
2-3 pounds red new potatoes

4-6 ears of corn, halved
¼ cup old bay seasoning
Cocktail sauce for serving

Place potatoes in a large pot with 3½ quarts of water. Bring to a boil and cook potatoes 5 minutes. Add old bay seasoning, sausage and corn. Cook 8-10 minutes until potatoes are tender. Add shrimp and continue to cook until shrimp is just cooked through and pink, 3-5 minutes. Remove from boiling water with a slotted spoon onto a large platter and serve with cocktail sauce.

GRILLED SALMON TACOS

serves 4 to 6

It's no secret that I love salmon and could literally eat it every day of the week. I am always finding new, creative ways to serve it. It is also no secret that I love fish tacos. This fresh combination bursts with flavor. The crisp salmon, soft tortilla, fresh avocado and spicy srirancha will tantilize the senses.

1 large salmon filet, 2-3 lbs.

1 tablespoon extra virgin olive oil

½ - 1 tablespoon kosher salt *(or course sea salt~Pink Himalayan)*

1 teaspoon fresh course ground pepper

1 teaspoon dried oregano

6-8 soft flour tortillas

8 oz. spring mix lettuces

Avocado salsa *(recipe to follow)*

Srirancha lime sauce *(recipe to follow)*

Heat grill or grill pan on cooktop to high heat. Brush both sides of salmon with olive oil and season with salt, pepper and oregano. Grill flesh side first until browned, then turn to skin side down. Reduce heat to medium low and close lid on grill (or cover loosely with foil) until fish has cooked through to desired temperature, 10-15 minutes. Remove to cutting board and cover loosely with foil to rest. Meanwhile, lay tortillas on grill to heat, one minute per side and place on a serving plate. Top each tortilla with a bed of the lettuce in its center. Cut the fish into strips and lay on top of lettuces. Spoon salsa over the salmon and finish with a drizzle of sauce over each taco. Garnish with a sprig of fresh cilantro.

avocado salsa

1 tablespoon fresh cilantro, finely chopped

1 large avocado, cut into 1-inch pieces

1 cup grape tomatoes, quartered

Zest and juice of ½ lemon

Zest and juice of ½ lime

1 tablespoon shallot, finely minced

1 tablespoon extra virgin olive oil

Dried oregano, course sea salt and ground pepper to taste

Combine all ingredients in small bowl and gently stir to combine flavors. Spoon over salmon.

the sauce

1 cup mayonaise

2 tablespoons Srirancha (red chili sauce)

1 tablespoon lime zest

1 tablespoon fresh lime juice

1 tablespoon fresh cilantro, finely chopped

Stir together all ingredients in a small bowl until smooth and creamy. Spoon over tacos.

LOBSTER FLATBREAD

Fresh flatbreads prepared with your favorite toppings are nothing short of fabulous. I love the explosive combination of flavors on this lobster flatbread. The secret is the cilantro pesto. I like to use my own flatbread (recipe to follow) when I have time but there is nothing wrong with store bought flatbreads or prepared pizza dough to save time without compromising flavor.

1 recipe flatbread dough or two balls prepared pizza dough (or store bought flatbreads)

1-2 grilled or broiled lobster tails, cut into 1 inch pieces (see recipe)
–OR–
½ lb. grilled shrimp cut in 1 inch pieces, (see recipe Rosemary Grilled Shrimp)

2 tablespoons extra virgin olive oil (for brushing dough)

Cilantro pesto (see recipe)

1 cup shredded mozzarella cheese

½ cup fontina cheese, thinly sliced

½ cup Parmigiano Reggiano cheese, grated

½ cup fresh basil leaves, julienne

1 tablespoon lemon zest

Sea salt and fresh ground pepper to taste

the flatbread

¾ cup warm water

1 envelope active dry yeast

2 cups all purpose organic flour

1 teaspoon sugar

¾ teaspoon kosher salt

3 tablespoons extra virgin olive oil

Combine water and yeast in a small bowl and let sit for 5 minutes. Meanwhile, place flour, sugar, salt, and olive oil in food processor. Add water-yeast mixture and pulse until dough forms into a ball. Knead on a floured surface (I like to use a pastry mat) for just a minute or two, until the dough is smooth. Place in a lightly oiled medium bowl and cover with plastic wrap. Allow to rise for 1 hour. Punch the dough and roll out lightly with a rolling pin into a disk shape. Divide into 4 equal pieces. If you are only using 2 flatbreads, wrap the other 2 disks well and freeze for a later use. Roll the dough into rounds, about ⅛ inch thick. Place on a pizza stone, sheet pan or directly on the grate of a gas or charcoal grill. Brush with extra virgin olive oil and bake 5 minutes in a 450 degree oven, or 1-2 minutes per side on the grill, at medium high heat, just until the edges begin to brown. Remove and prepare with toppings.

Spoon cilantro pesto in the center of each flatbread spreading evenly with a spoon or pastry brush leaving a 1-inch border around the edges. Top with lobster pieces laying fontina slices over top.

Generously sprinkle with mozzarella and grated Parmigiano Reggiano. Season with salt, pepper to taste and top with fresh basil, reserving some for finishing. Drizzle the flat breads with extra virgin olive oil and bake for an additional 5-7 minutes until heated through and the cheese is bubbly. Finish with fresh lemon zest and more fresh basil leaves.

cilantro pesto

1 tablespoon lemon zest
1 tablespoon fresh lemon juice
1 cup fresh cilantro leaves
1 cup fresh basil leaves

½ cup walnut pieces, toasted
½ cup extra virgin olive oil
½ teaspoon each kosher salt and fresh ground pepper to taste

Toast walnuts on a sheet pan in a 350 degree oven until lightly browned, approximately 10 minutes. Allow to cool to room temperature. Place cilantro, basil, walnuts, lemon juice, lemon zest, salt and pepper in food processor. In a gentle stream, add olive oil one tablespoon at a time until thoroughly combined. Remove pesto to a bowl and stir in Parmigiano Reggiano. Add more salt and pepper to taste if desired.

serves 4 to 6

LOBSTER MARTINI

This sophisticated and decadent appetizer could just as well be an elegant meal. Served in a martini glass alongside a tall chilled flute of bubbly, I can't think of a more beautiful way to start...or finish! You can boil the lobsters yourself, or have your fish monger steam them for you, making this fabulous dish so simple to prepare.

2-3 whole steamed Maine lobsters,
(1 to 1½ pounds each)

2 cups dry white wine

Lemony Chevre Mashed Potatoes
(see accompaniments & tasteful sides)

½ cup extra virgin olive oil

1 tablespoon fresh lemon juice

1 tablespoon fresh lemon zest

1 tablespoon fresh orange zest

1 teaspoon fresh lime juice

1 tablespoon fresh lime zest

2 tablespoons fresh tarragon, chopped

1 tablespoon fresh chives, finely chopped

1 teaspoon course sea salt

Whole chive sprigs for garnish

Prepare lemony mashed potatoes (see recipe, pg. 160) and keep warm in a covered bowl over a pot of simmering water, or simply re-heat in the microwave just before assembling the martinis. In a medium bowl, whisk together olive oil, juices, zest, tarragon, chives and sea salt. Set aside.

If you decide to cook your own lobsters, fill a large pot with 2 cups dry white wine and enough water to cover the lobsters. Bring to a boil. Add the lobsters, head first, and cover. When the water has regained a rolling boil, reduce heat to medium high and cook lobsters for 10-15 minutes longer. Using tongs remove the lobsters from boiling water to a platter. While still warm, but cool enough to handle, remove tails and claws. Carefully remove claw meat from the shells, keeping the meat in tact. Remove meat from tail, and cut into bite size pieces, 1-2 inch chunks. Remove roe from body, rinsing well and save for another use, along with shells (bisque, stew, paella, cioppino). This can be frozen for up to 3 months, or simply discard.

Add lobster tail meat to the citrus and herb vinaigrette and toss to combine. Divide potatoes among martini glasses and spoon lobster tail, citrus mixture over potatoes. Place meat from one claw in each glass. Sprinkle with chopped chives and garnish with whole chive sprigs. Serve with a tall chilled flute of champagne.

ROSEMARY GRILLED SHRIMP COCKTAIL

Living in the South Carolina Low Country, fresh shrimp are plentiful and so delicious. I use this simple shrimp recipe in a variety of dishes, or as a stand alone appetizer. So easy to prepare and takes very little time. Fresh and flavorful, this dish pairs well with a salad or pasta with a citrus vinaigrette.

1 lb. fresh cocktail size shrimp, 15-20 count, shells and vein removed, tails remain

Juice and zest of one medium orange

1 cup extra virgin olive oil

8 rosemary sprigs,

2 tablespoons fresh rosemary leaves, finely chopped

Dash kosher salt and freshly ground pepper to taste

1 tablespoon fresh lemon zest *(for serving)*

Starting 2 inches from the top of each rosemary sprig, remove leaves with your fingers, exposing the sprig, which will be used as a skewer to cook the shrimp. Finely chop rosemary leaves and place in a small bowl with olive oil, ¼ cup freshly squeezed orange juice, orange zest, salt and pepper. Whisk until well combined and pour over shrimp. Toss to coat evenly. While the shrimp is marinating, spray grill or grill pan (on cooktop) with non-stick spray and bring to medium high heat. Skewer shrimp on rosemary sprigs and grill until just cooked through, 1-2 minutes per side. Serve on rosemary skewers with cocktail sauce as an appetizer, or over a mixed green salad with citrus vinaigrette. Finish with a sprinkling of chopped rosemary leaves and lemon zest.

cocktail sauce

I like to add a little zing to the cocktail sauce to compliment the shrimp. Start with 1-2 cups of your favorite cocktail sauce and add 1-2 teaspoons of orange zest, 1-2 teaspoons finely chopped rosemary leaves and 1 teaspoon organic honey. Stir until well combined and serve with the shrimp. If you like a little heat in your sauce, a jigger of Texas Pete (or more to taste) will finish it perfectly!

citrus vinaigrette

¾ cup extra virgin olive oil

1 tablespoon fresh lemon juice

1 tablespoon fresh squeezed orange juice

1 teaspoon each lemon and orange zest

1 teaspoon dried oregano

1 teaspoon organic honey

Course sea salt and fresh ground pepper to taste

Whisk all ingredients together in a small bowl until thoroughly combined and emulsified.

serves 4 to 6

SCALLOPS MARNIER

This delicious appetizer is rich and sweet, but feels light on the palette. The scallops are crispy, yet juicy, a beautiful compliment with the lavishness of the orange scented sauce. You will find a similar recipe in the pasta section to serve as a lunch or dinner entree served over capellini.

16-24 medium bay scallops, rinsed well and dried thoroughly with paper towels
½ cup Grand Marnier (*orange liqueur*)
¼ cup unsalted butter
¼ cup flat leaf parsley, chopped

1 tablespoon fresh orange zest
½ cup fresh chives, finely chopped
Course sea salt and fresh ground pepper to taste
Fresh chives for garnish

Heat 1 tablespoon olive oil in a large sauté pan over medium high heat. Season scallops with course sea salt and pepper and sear until deep golden brown on both sides, approximately 3 minutes per side. Remove from pan and cover with foil to rest and keep warm while you prepare the sauce.

the sauce

Deglaze the pan with orange liqueur over medium high heat stirring the browned bits from the bottom of the pan. Bring to a simmer allowing the alcohol to steam off, 1-2 minutes. Add butter and reduce heat to medium low. When the butter has completely melted and incorporated into the sauce, add the parsley and orange zest. Stir to combine.

Spoon ⅓ of the sauce on individual appetizer serving plates and arrange 3-4 scallops on top of the sauce on each plate. Spoon remaining sauce over scallops and sprinkle with fresh chopped chives. Garnish with a few whole chives.

Bread PASTA & RISOTTO

RUSTIC ITALIAN LOAF

One of the most comforting aromas coming from the kitchen is the smell of fresh bread baking. This rustic Italian loaf is brown and wonderfully crusty on the outside and light and spongy on the inside. Perfect for soaking up a good dipping oil, pasta sauce or even creamy butter.

5½ cups organic bread flour
1 packet active dry yeast
3 cups warm water

1 tablespoon extra virgin olive oil
1 tablespoon kosher salt

In the bowl of an electric stand mixer add 2 cups of flour, yeast, and salt. Mix well using the dough hook attachment. Add water and olive oil and mix on low speed until well combined. Add 2 more cups of flour and mix well. Add remaining flour and mix. Sprinkle a little flour on top of the dough and cover with a kitchen towel. Let the dough rise for 1½ hours. This process can also be done by hand using a wooden spoon to mix. Pour dough out onto floured surface and cut into 2 equal parts. Using your hands, shape each to form a loaf and place on a sheet pan. Cover with a kitchen towel and allow the dough to rise another 30 minutes. In the meantime, preheat the oven to 450 degrees.

Spritz the oven with water from a misting bottle and immediately put the bread in the oven. Bake for 30-35 minutes until dark brown and crusty out the outside and sounds hollow when tapped. Cool completely on wire racks. Serve at room temperature or reheated in a 425 degree oven for 5-10 minutes.

You can also slice the bread, brush with extra virgin olive oil and toast under the broiler or grill until golden brown and crispy on the edges and still spongy on the inside.

makes 2 loaves

FRESH PASTA

There is nothing to be afraid of in making your own pasta. It is simple and doesn't take much time or require a lot of work. I use my Kitchen Aide stand mixer and pasta attachment, it is so worth the investment! My idea of a perfect Sunday afternoon is in the kitchen making pasta!

4 cups pasta flour *(a blend of all purpose flour and semolina. I like King Arthur Flour, Pasta Flour Blend)*

5 organic eggs

1 tablespoon **extra virgin olive oil**

1 tablespoon **course sea salt** *(or kosher salt)*

Place flour in the bowl of stand mixer and make a well in the middle. In a small bowl, whisk together eggs, olive oil and salt. Pour into well of flour and mix on low speed with paddle attachment until dough begins to form. Pour dough out onto a floured surface and form into a ball. Lightly flour the dough and knead until smooth, 5 minutes. Pat and shape the dough into an oblong disk and wrap with plastic wrap. Allow the dough to rest at least 30 minutes at room temperature.

After it has rested, you can roll and cut the dough, or refrigerate for several hours or overnight. It also freezes very well. To thaw, bring from the freezer to the refrigerator until you are ready to roll into sheets and cut into your preferred pasta.

Cut a small amount of dough (approximately 3-4 inches) from the disk. Work the dough with your fingers into a flat disk and lightly flour on both sides. With the pasta attachment, begin feeding the dough through the rollers at level 1 on low speed ("stir"). Fold the dough in half or thirds and run through on level 1 again. Repeat this 5 times, until the dough is smooth, then run through once on each level until reaching level 6. Lay pasta sheets on a floured non-stick surface.

serves 4 to 6

fettucine

Run the pasta sheets through the Fettucine cutter attachment, or fold pasta sheet over on both sides (into thirds) and cut with a knife to desired noodle thickness. Lightly flour the pasta sheets prior to folding and cutting to prevent the pasta from sticking together. Then simply cut to desired noodle thickness, Fettucine *(as shown)* or Papparadelle *(wider noodle)*.

Helpful Hint ~
The use of a lightly floured non-stick pastry mat makes a great surface for working with pasta. I use one for kneading, laying out the pasta sheets, and also cutting. *Sur La Table* offers a wonderful large pastry mat that makes working pastry dough for pies, scones, biscuits, and cookie cut outs, with ease.

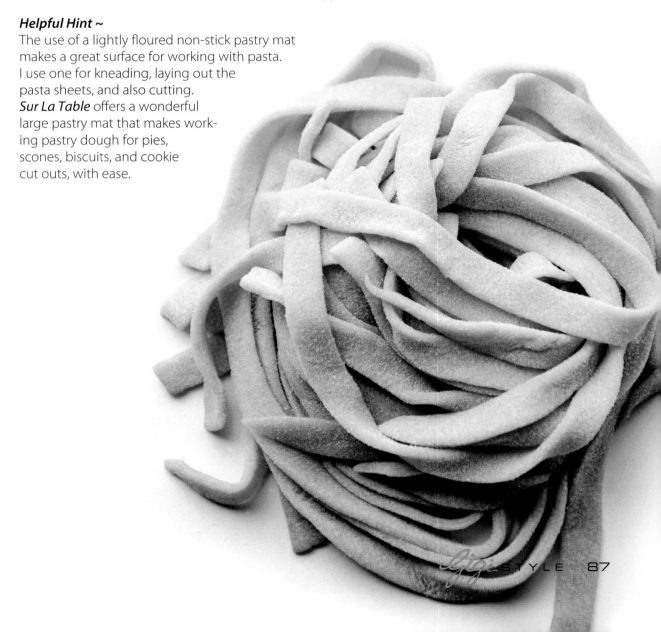

FETTUCINE ALFREDO

serves 2 to 4

Jeff's favorite pasta, bar none, he could eat it every day if I would let him! I start mine with a simple Bechamel and spice it up, Gigi style. It is rich and creamy with a hint of nutmeg and scent of lemon zest, which makes it taste light, but don't kid yourself it is all fredo!

½ **recipe fresh Fettucine or ½ lb. dried Fettucine** *(such as Cipriana or Barilla)*

2 tablespoons unsalted butter

2 tablespoons organic flour

2 cups milk at room temperature *(organic 2% milk fat)*

1 teaspoon kosher salt

½-1 teaspoon ground pepper

¼ **teaspoon ground nutmeg**

1 tablespoon lemon zest *(plus more for serving)*

½ **cup Parmigiano-Reggiano cheese, freshly grated** *(plus more for serving)*

1 tablespoon flat leaf *(Italian)* **parsley, chopped** *(plus more for serving)*

Bring 4 quarts of water to a boil. When the water begins to boil rapidly, add a pinch of kosher salt and then the pasta. Cook, stirring occasionally, for 5-7 minutes for fresh pasta, 8-10 minutes for dried pasta, to al dente consistency (firm to the bite).

Meanwhile, melt butter in a large sauté pan or braiser pan over medium heat. When the butter begins to foam sprinkle flour evenly into the butter and whisk until well combined. Continue to stir until the mixture begins to bubble, then, slowly add milk, whisking constantly until thoroughly combined with the flour mixture. Add salt, pepper, nutmeg and lemon zest and continue to stir until the sauce thickens. Stir in cheese. By this time, your pasta should be ready. Using a pasta spoon or tongs, bring pasta from water directly into the sauce, reserving the pasta water. Stir sauce and pasta together until well combined and add parsley.

Allow to cook for a minute or two for the pasta to absorb some of the sauce while it thickens. If your sauce appears to be too thick, add ¼-½ cup of the reserved pasta water and stir into the sauce and pasta mixture. Pour into a large serving bowl (or individual pasta bowls) and top with more grated cheese. Season with salt and pepper to taste and finish with a sprinkle of lemon zest and fresh chopped parsley.

Variation ~
For a more complete dish add some protein. Top with a sliced grilled chicken breast or salmon filet.

FETTUCINE CAPONATA

A perfect dish after a visit to the Farmers Market. One of my favorite vegetarian dishes, hearty and healthy. The roasted vegetables of the Caponata have so much flavor. Toss with my fresh pasta cut into Fettuccine or Pappardelle, or a dried version of either. This robust sauce calls for a wide and sturdy noodle.

1 lb. Fettuccine or Pappardelle
1 medium eggplant
1 medium zucchini
1 medium yellow squash
½ cup extra virgin olive oil
2 garlic cloves (minced)
2 tablespoons fresh thyme leaves
16 ounce can diced tomatoes
  (San Marzano)

2 tablespoons capers (drained)
½ cup kalamata olives, chopped
1 tablespoon fresh lemon zest
½ cup flat leaf parsley (chopped)
½ cup Parmigiano-Reggiano cheese
  (grated)
½ cup Pecorino Romano (grated)
Course sea salt and freshly ground
pepper to taste

Preheat oven to 425 degrees. Cut vegetables into 1 inch cubes and place in a roasting pan. Drizzle generously with extra virgin olive oil and thyme leaves, toss. Season with course sea salt (or kosher salt) and pepper. Roast until browned on the outside and tender on the inside, 15-20 minutes. Add tomatoes, capers, olives, lemon zest, and parsley, stir. Turn off the heat and return to the oven until the tomatoes are heated through, 5-7 minutes. Meanwhile, cook pasta to al dente, following package directions (or my fresh pasta recipe). With a pasta spoon or tongs, remove pasta to a serving bowl, reserving pasta water. Add the caponata of vegetables and cheeses to the pasta and toss well. Add pasta water in ¼ cup increments and stir into the pasta until the sauce reaches your desired consistency. Finish with more freshly grated cheese and a drizzle of extra virgin olive oil.

serves 4 to 6

LOBSTER MAC

If Merriam-Webster's French definition of decadence is *"luxurious self-indulgence,"* this dish is just that, **c'est la pure mac et la fromage de'cadence.** Rich and cheesy with lobster and creamy bechamel sauce. Mac and cheese doesn't get any better!

4 cups cooked lobster meat *(see recipes~what's for dinner)*

1 lb. Cavatappi pasta *(or medium shells)*

6 ounces Fontina cheese, thinly sliced

6 ounces Gruyere cheese, grated

6 ounces raw sharp cheddar cheese, grated

1 cup Parmigiano-Reggiano cheese, finely grated

3 tablespoons flat leaf parsley, finely chopped

½ cup bread crumbs.

1 teaspoon lemon zest

Bechamel sauce *(recipe to follow)*

Preheat oven to 375 degrees. Cook pasta according to package directions. Meanwhile, prepare Bechamel sauce. When sauce is thick, add Fontina, Gruyere, half of the cheddar, and ½ cup of the Parmigiano-Reggiano cheese, stirring until melted. Add 2 tablespoons of the parsley and lemon zest. Using a spider or slotted spoon, transfer the cooked pasta directly from pasta water into the sauce, reserving cooking liquid. Stir to combine. If sauce appears to be too thick, add a little pasta water, ¼ cup at a time. Spray non-stick spray in a large baking dish or 3½ quart oval Dutch oven, and pour the pasta with sauce into prepared dish. You can also prepare in individual serving ramekins. Spread remaining cheddar evenly over the top. In a small bowl, combine bread crumbs, remaining ½ cup of grated Parmigiano-Reggiano cheese and 1 tablespoon parsley. Sprinkle over the top of the pasta and drizzle with extra virgin olive oil. Bake 40-50 minutes until nicely browned on top and cheese is bubbling around the edges (30 minutes for individual ramekins). Allow to rest 5-10 minutes before serving. Finish with more fresh chopped parsley and grated Parmigiano-Reggiano if desired.

bechamel sauce

¼ cup unsalted butter

¼ cup all purpose flour

4 cups warm milk *(2% is fine)*

1 teaspoon kosher salt

½ teaspoon fresh ground pepper

½ teaspoon freshly grated *(or ground)* **nutmeg**

In a large sauté pan (3-4 quart) melt butter over medium heat. Sprinkle flour over butter and whisk until well combined and flour has dissolved into the butter. Slowly add warm milk and continue to stir with whisk until the sauce begins to thicken and sticks to the back of a spoon. Stir in salt, pepper and nutmeg.

serves 6 to 8

PAGLIA e FIENO

Paglia e Fieno, translated *"hay and straw,"* is an ultra-rich, creamy and luxurious combination of plain pasta (hay) and spinach pasta (straw) originating in the northern regions of Italy. The delicate balance of the velvety textured sauce and salty bite of the prosciutto are a match made in pasta heaven. I like using a combination of dried linguine (regular and spinach) for this dish, though fresh plain and spinach fettucine are also amazing in this lush and savory sauce.

½ pound dried linguine

½ pound dried spinach linguine

2 tablespoons unsalted butter

1 tablespoon flour

2 cups milk, room temperature
   (2% milk fat)

1 cup heavy cream, room temperature

1 teaspoon kosher salt

1 teaspoon freshly ground pepper

¼ teaspoon ground nutmeg

½ cup Parmigiano-Reggiano cheese,
   freshly grated *(plus more for serving)*

1 tablespoon flat leaf parsley, chopped
   (plus more for serving)

¼ pound prosciutto, chopped

1 tablespoon fresh lemon zest
   (for serving)

Bring 4 quarts of water to a boil. When the water begins to boil rapidly, add a pinch of kosher salt and then the pasta. Cook to al dente consistency (firm to the bite) according to package directions. Meanwhile, melt butter in a large sauté pan or braiser pan over medium heat. When the butter begins to foam, sprinkle the flour evenly into the butter and whisk until well combined. Continue to stir until the mixture begins to bubble, then slowly add the milk, whisking constantly until all of the milk is well combined with the flour mixture. When the sauce begins to thicken, add cream, salt, pepper and nutmeg, and continue to stir until the sauce thickens. Stir in cheese, prosciutto and parsley. By this time, the pasta should be ready. Using a pasta spoon or tongs, bring pasta directly from cooking liquid into the sauce, reserving the pasta water. Stir sauce and pasta together until well combined.

Allow to cook for a minute or two while the sauce continues to thicken and the pasta absorbs some of the sauce. If the sauce appears to be too thick, add ¼- ½ cup of the reserved pasta water and stir into the sauce and pasta mixture. Pour into a large pasta serving bowl or individual pasta bowls using tongs and top with more grated cheese and salt and pepper to taste. Finish with a sprinkle of fresh lemon zest and flat leaf parsley.

serves 4 to 6

SCALLOPS MARNIER OVER CAPELLINI

A lovely lunch entrée or pasta course appetizer for a larger meal or three-course dinner party. This dish is rich and sweet, but feels light on the palette. The crispy yet juicy scallops are a beautiful compliment with the lavishness of the orange scented sauce.

serves 4 to 6

16-24 medium bay scallops, rinsed well
¾ pound Capellini or thin spaghetti
½ cup Grand Marnier *(orange liqueur)*
1 cup fresh squeezed orange juice
¼ cup unsalted butter
¼ cup flat leaf parsley, chopped
1 tablespoon fresh orange zest
Gremolata of Parmigiano-Reggiano cheese, orange zest, & flat leaf parsley

Heat 1 tablespoon olive oil in a large sauté pan over medium high heat. Season scallops with course sea salt and pepper and lightly toss in flour. Sear until deep golden brown on both sides, 2-3 minutes per side. Remove from pan and cover with foil to keep warm. In the same sauté pan, prepare the sauce. Meanwhile, bring a large pot of water to a boil. Add 1 teaspoon kosher salt and the Capellini. Cook according to package directions. With a pasta spoon or tongs, add the pasta to the sauce and toss to coat. Add scallops, spooning excess sauce over them. Simmer while the pasta absorbs the flavors of the sauce, 3-5 minutes. Pour into a large serving bowl or spoon into individual pasta bowls. Finish with a gremolata of freshly grated Parmigiano-Reggiano cheese, orange zest and chopped flat leaf parsley.

the sauce

After removing scallops, deglaze the pan with orange liqueur over medium heat stirring the browned bits from the bottom of the pan. Bring to a bubbly simmer allowing the alcohol to cook off, 1-2 minutes. Add orange juice and continue to simmer until liquid has reduced in half. Add butter and reduce heat to medium low. When the butter has completely melted and incorporated into the sauce, add the parsley and orange zest. Stir to combine.

the gremolata

**1 cup Parmigiano-Reggiano
   cheese, grated**
1 tablespoon orange zest

**2 tablespoons flat leaf parsley,
   finely chopped**

Combine all ingredients in a small bowl. Toss with fingertips until well combined.

PUMPKIN RAVIOLI

When fall arrives, I can't wait to cook with the flavors of the season, especially pumpkin. This warm aromatic dish will melt in your mouth and soothe your soul. Perfect for a crisp fall evening as an appetizer or main course topped with my rosemary grilled shrimp and arugula side salad.

serves 6 to 8

1 recipe fresh pasta, rolled into sheets *(to setting #6, or 1 package wonton wrappers)*

1 small bowl of water

1 cup pumpkin puree, organic

1 cup Parmigiano-Reggiano cheese, finely grated

1 cup Amaretti cookies *(or ginger snaps)* finely grated in food processor

1 teaspoon lemon zest

Pinch of kosher salt

¼ teaspoon freshly ground pepper

¼ teaspoon freshly ground nutmeg *(fresh preferably but not necessary)*

¼ cup flat leaf parsley, finely chopped

1 cup toasted walnuts, rough chop

More Parmigiano-Reggiano cheese, finely grated for serving

Assembly ~

Prepare pasta sheets. If you are using wonton wrappers, cover with a damp paper towel to keep them from drying out while assembling the ravioli. In a medium bowl, stir together pumpkin, cheese, and cookies, then, add lemon zest, salt, pepper, nutmeg and 2 teaspoons of the parsley, stirring until well combined. Using a floured non-stick pastry mat as your work surface, take one pasta sheet at a time and dollop spoonfuls of filling in a row down the center of your pasta sheet, about 2 inches apart. With a pastry brush, brush water on the pasta around each dollop of filling out to the edges. This will be the glue that holds the ravioli together. Lay a second pasta sheet directly on top and work your fingers around each dollop, sealing the two pasta sheets together. Be sure to work out any air bubbles that may have gotten in between the sheets during the process. Using a ravioli cutter, divide your ravioli, then cut along the top and sides of the pasta sheets, further sealing each ravioli. Carefully remove to a cutting board that fits on the shelf in your freezer.

Freeze the ravioli for 15-20 minutes, then, they can be placed in Ziploc bags and stored in the freezer for up to one month. When you are ready to cook, take directly from the freezer to boiling water. If you are using wonton wrappers, it's the same process, you will just be making only one ravioli at a time. Bring a large pot of water to a boil and add a pinch of salt. Gently drop ravioli into the boiling water and stir to prevent from sticking to the bottom until the water returns to a boil. Cook 2-3 minutes, just until the pasta is cooked and the filling is heated through. Remove ravioli with a slotted spoon directly to a serving platter or individual serving plates. Spoon sauce over each ravioli and finish with grated Parmigiano-Reggiano cheese, toasted walnuts and a sprinkling of lemon zest and finely chopped parsley.

the sauce

½ cup unsalted butter

1 tablespoon extra virgin olive oil

¼ cup fresh sage leaves, julienne

½ teaspoon freshly grated nutmeg

Melt butter over medium low heat until it begins to foam. Add olive oil and stir. Add sage leaves, nutmeg and allow the aromatics to infuse into the sauce for one minute, remove from heat. Spoon over ravioli and top with toasted walnuts, freshly grated Parmigiano-Reggiano cheese, and a sprinkling of lemon zest, grated nutmeg and fresh ground pepper.

BASIC TRADITIONAL RISOTTO

A Gigi specialty. One of the dishes that my dinner guests ask for time and time again. Risotto is so versatile and can be served in a multitude of variations, all starting with this basic risotto. Creamy and delicious with just enough bite. A northern Italian traditional first course, this basic recipe is all you need for a wonderful side dish or main course with a few added ingredients.

2 cups good Italian Arborio rice

2 tablespoons unsalted butter *(separated)*

1 medium shallot, minced

½ cup dry white wine

4-6 cups chicken or vegetable stock *(or good organic low sodium broth)*

1 teaspoon kosher salt

1 teaspoon freshly ground pepper

1 cup Parmigiano-Reggiano cheese, grated, plus extra for serving

1 tablespoon flat leaf parsley, chopped plus extra for serving

1 teaspoon grated zest of lemon

1 teaspoon fresh lemon juice *(or more to taste)*

1 teaspoon white truffle oil *(optional)*

Chiffonade of fresh basil leaves to finish *(optional)*

Place stock or broth in a medium saucepan over medium low heat. Melt 1 tablespoon unsalted butter in a risotto pan or Dutch oven over medium heat. Add shallot and cook until soft, 5-7 minutes. Add rice and stir to coat well. Add wine and stir continuously until all of the wine has been absorbed by the rice. Increase heat to medium high, and begin adding broth with a ladle, ½ cup at a time while continuing to stir with each addition until all of the broth has been absorbed, 20-30 minutes. Risotto will be plump, slightly al dente and creamy. Stir in cheese, parsley and lemon. Season with salt and pepper and add remaining tablespoon of unsalted butter, stirring until melted. Stir in truffle oil if desired and season with more salt and pepper to taste. Spoon risotto into a large serving bowl or individual serving bowls. Finish with more freshly grated Parmigiano-Reggiano, fresh chopped parsley and/or basil and a drizzle of good extra virgin olive oil.

risotto milanese

Simply add a generous pinch of saffron threads to the risotto while you are adding stock or broth. The saffron will dissolve beautifully into the risotto, turning it a bright "saffron yellow" in color and richness in flavor. The perfect compliment to my *Veal Ossobuco*!

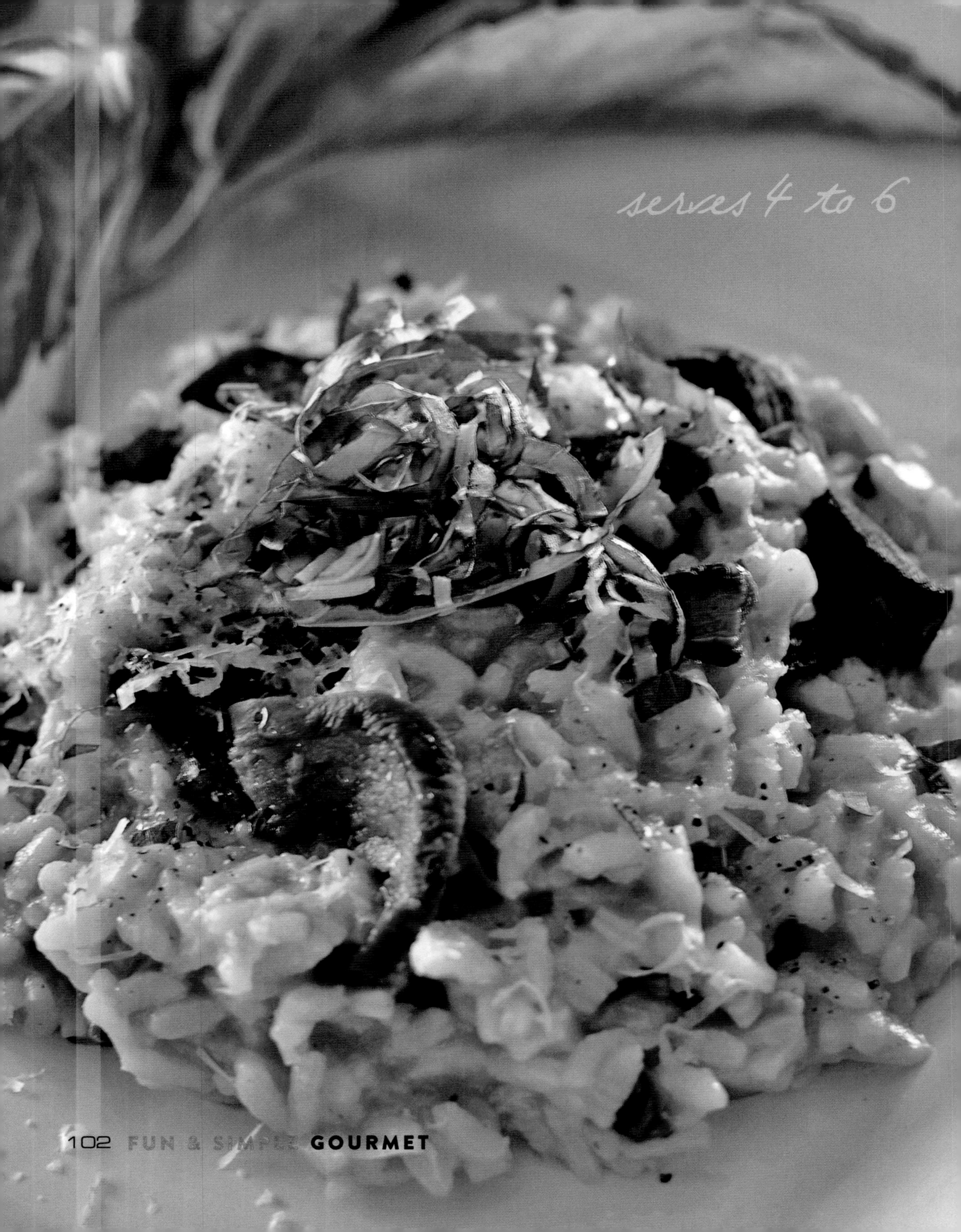

serves 4 to 6

BASIC OVEN RISOTTO

Being somewhat of a risotto traditionalist, I was reluctant to try the oven method, but you will be astonished at just how flawlessly this risotto performs. It is ideal for a dinner party as you don't have to be in the kitchen stirring for 30 minutes, you can enjoy your guests practically until serving time. Rich, creamy, nearly effortless.

2 tablespoons unsalted butter

1 small onion or medium shallot, finely chopped

1 cup Arborio Rice

½ cup dry white wine

2¾ cups chicken stock, heated
(or organic low sodium vegetable or chicken broth)

2 cups grated Parmigiano-Reggiano cheese

1 tablespoon flat leaf parsley, chopped

Fresh basil leaves, julienne

1 teaspoon fresh lemon zest

Kosher salt and fresh ground pepper to taste

Preheat oven to 350 degrees. Melt butter in a Dutch oven, *(I like my LeCreuset oval dutch oven)* over medium heat. Add onion and cook until soft, stirring constantly so the onion does not burn or stick to the bottom of the pan. Add rice and stir well to coat the rice evenly with the butter. Season with salt and pepper and cook for about 5 minutes, continuing to stir. Add wine and simmer, continuing to stir until all of the wine has been absorbed. Add 2 cups warm broth, and bring to a simmer. Cover tightly with lid and place in the oven, 15-18 minutes, or until all of the liquid is absorbed. Remove cover and bring the rice to the cooktop. Just prior to serving, add the remaining ¾ cup broth and cook over medium heat stirring until the rice is tender and creamy, 3-5 minutes. Stir in one more tablespoon unsalted butter, Parmigiano-Reggiano cheese, parsley and lemon zest. Season to taste with salt and pepper and pour into a serving bowl. Serve immediately with more grated Parmigiano-Reggiano cheese and julienne of fresh basil.

porcini mushroom risotto

1 cup dried porcini mushrooms
White Truffle Oil

Soak 1 cup dried porcini mushrooms in water to hydrate, 20-30 minutes. Drain and rinse well. Set aside. When the risotto has absorbed the last ¾ cup broth, add the porcini to the risotto along with the butter, cheese and herbs. Stir to combine and allow the porcini to heat through while the cheese melts into the risotto. Season with course sea salt and fresh ground pepper to taste. To enhance the mushroom flavor and add a hint of decadence, finish with a scant drizzle of white truffle oil. Stir into the risotto and pour into a serving bowl. Serve immediately with more grated cheese and julienne of fresh basil leaves. A hearty and rich main course risotto.

Hey!
WHAT'S FOR
DINNER?

What's for Dinner…the age-old question.

Take the stress out of the answer by letting these simple dinner suggestions be your guide. You will find many common techniques that can transform any dish to *simply spectacular* with very little time or even effort, **Gigi Style** the "***fun & simple gourmet***" way, making what's for dinner a pleasure.

Whether cooking for just the two of you, your entire family, or entertaining a crowd, these beautifully easy entrées will make a hit every time!

FRESH LOBSTER TAILS

You will find these succulent tails in many of my lobster recipes. So simple to prepare in so many delicious and creative ways from simply grilled or broiled as a main course entrée to an elegant lobster benedict brunch. Here are the basics for cooking perfect lobster tails. I like to serve with my *lemony chevre mashed potatoes, roasted asparagus* and chilled prosecco or champagne. So easy, so exquisite! Serve with drawn butter and lemon wedges.

8-ounce spiny lobster tails
(1 tail per person)

Extra virgin olive oil

Course sea salt *(I love pink Himalayan sea salt with lobster)*

Course ground black pepper

Sprigs of fresh rosemary and/or fresh thyme *(optional)*

½ cup *(1 stick)* **melted drawn butter with garlic and lemon**

Fresh lemon wedges *(for serving)*

broiling or grilling

Preheat broiler to 500 degrees or grill to high heat. Using kitchen shears, cut the shell of the lobster down the middle to the fan tail. Turn over and cut the ribs of the tail. Holding with the shell side on top, crack the shell apart, carefully, keeping the meat of the tail in tact. Rinse and remove center vein, dry thoroughly on paper towels. Place lobster tails on sheet pan and drizzle with good extra virgin olive oil. Season with course sea salt and freshly ground black pepper. For added flavor, lay a spring of fresh rosemary and/or fresh thyme down the center of each tail. Place sheet pan under broiler, 6 inches from heat. Cook until lobster tails begin to brown on the edges and the center appears opaque, 5-7 minutes. Turn the heat off and close the oven door or grill lid to allow the tails to cook through, no more than 5 minutes longer. Be very careful not to overcook! Melt one stick of butter slowly in small saucepan over medium low heat with one smashed garlic clove and 1 teaspoon fresh lemon juice. When ready to serve, remove garlic clove and pour into a small sauce boat or spouted serving dish.

Serve for dinner with my *lemony chevre mashed potatoes* and *roasted asparagus.*

grilling ~ (shell on)

Jeff's favorite way to prepare the lobster tails. Using kitchen shears, cut the shell of the lobster down the middle to the fan tail. Holding with the shell side on top, crack the shell apart slightly and remove center vein. Blot meat dry with paper towels. Drizzle each tail with good extra virgin olive oil and a squeeze of fresh lemon juice. Season with course sea salt and freshly ground black pepper. Place on the grill, meat side down until lobster tails begin to brown. Turn over, reduce heat to low and place tails away from the flame, either on the other side of the grill or an upper shelf. Close lid of grill allowing lobster to cook through, approximately 7-10 minutes. The center will appear opaque. Keep an eye on the tails as they finish to prevent overcooking.

WHOLE STEAMED LOBSTER

Whole steamed Maine lobsters are a special treat because of the wonderful sweet and tender claw meat, which you don't have with spiny lobsters from southern waters. Steaming lobster in white wine helps to tenderize the meat and adds such nice flavor. Though most of my lobster dishes use grilled or broiled lobster tails, you will find whole steamed lobster in my *Lobster Martini Appetizer* recipe where the claw is key!

2 or 3 whole Maine lobsters,
  (1 to 1½ lbs. each)
2 cups dry white wine
1 tablespoon course sea salt
  or kosher salt

1 cup butter, melted
1 garlic clove, smashed
Lemon wedges, for serving
Course sea salt and freshly ground
  pepper to taste

Fill a large pot with 2 cups dry white wine, 1 tablespoon salt, and enough water to cover the lobsters. Bring to a boil. Add the lobsters, head first, and cover. When the water has regained a rolling boil, reduce heat to medium high and cook lobsters for 10-15 minutes longer. While the lobsters are cooking, place 1 cup butter and 1 smashed garlic clove in a small sauce pan and melt over medium low heat until completely melted and just beginning to appear foamy.

When the lobsters have finished cooking, use tongs to remove them from the boiling water to a board and allow to cool enough to handle. If you want to serve without having your guests work for their lobster, remove tails and claws by chopping at the joints with a cleaver or large sharp knife. Carefully remove the meat from the claws using a mallet to crack through the shells, keeping the meat in tact. Cut the shell of the tails with kitchen shears down the center of the tail and remove tail meat. Place on a serving platter and season with salt and pepper. Remove roe from body, rinsing well and save for another use, which can be frozen along with the shells for up to 3 months, or simply discard.

Or, simply split the lobsters lengthwise, shell side down, remove roe and place the halved steamed lobsters on a serving platter. Season meat with salt and pepper and bring to the table with mallets letting everyone crack their own...fun and simple!

Serve with melted drawn butter and lemon wedges.

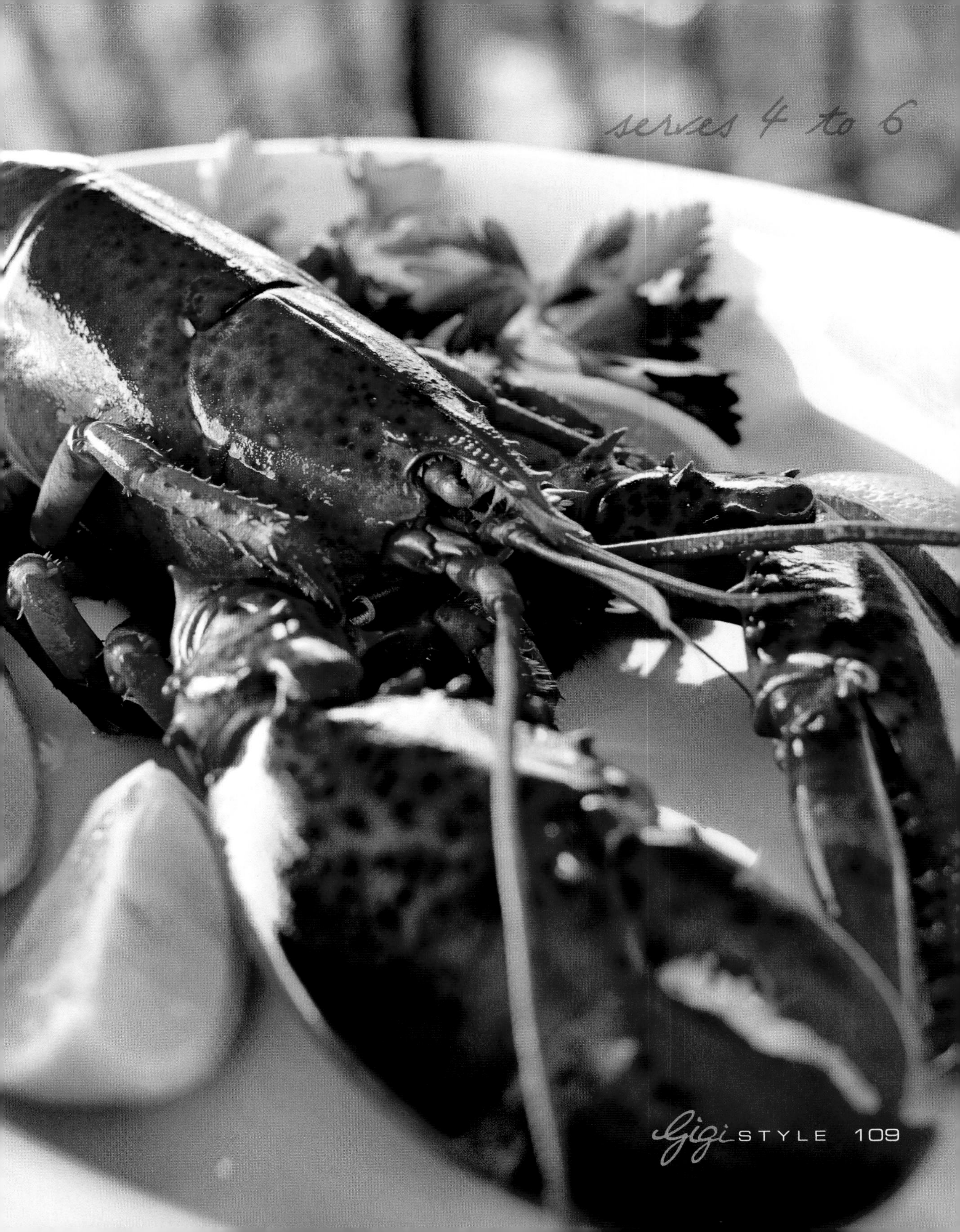

serves 4 to 6

CALAMARI POMODORO

This tender sautéed calamari, a traditional Southern Italian dish originating from Naples, is perfect on its own with crusty ciabatta bread for dipping in its savory sauce, or tossed with fettucine or linguine. Calamari, which means *inkwell* from the Greek word, "*calamos*," is very common in Mediterranean cuisine.

Serve with my **lemony caesar salad** and **crusty ciabatta bread**...simply divine!

2 pounds squid *(calamari)*, rinsed well

¼ cup extra virgin olive oil, plus more for serving

1 medium shallot, thinly sliced

4 garlic cloves, minced

1 teaspoon red pepper flakes

½ cup dry white wine

2 cups tomato puree or crushed tomatoes *(canned San Marzano or fresh roma tomatoes blanched and pureed in blender)*

1 teaspoon dried oregano

1 tablespoon fresh lemon juice

1 tablespoon lemon zest

1 cup pitted Kalamata olives

½ cup flat leaf parsley

½ cup Parmigiano-Reggiano Cheese, finely grated

Course sea salt and fresh ground pepper to taste

Rinse squid well and dry with paper towels. Slice tubes into 1 to 1½ inch rings. Set aside. Place olive oil in a large sauté pan over medium heat. Add shallot and cook until soft, 3-5 minutes. Add garlic and red pepper and cook no more than one minute. Stir in tomatoes, white wine, salt, pepper and oregano and simmer until the sauce begins to thicken, 10-15 minutes. Add lemon juice, lemon zest, olives and squid and continue to simmer until the squid is just cooked through, 2-3 minutes. Be careful not to overcook the squid.

Spoon into individual serving bowls and finish with a sprinkling of fresh flat leaf parsley, freshly grated Parmigiano-Reggiano cheese and lemon zest. Drizzle with good extra virgin olive oil and serve with my *Lemony Caesar Salad* and crusty Italian bread for dipping in the savory sauce.

variation~ *serving with fettucine or linguine*

Cook ¾ pound pasta according to package directions. When the squid is cooked through, bring pasta directly from pasta water into the sauté pan with tongs or a pasta spoon. Add Parmigiano-Reggiano cheese and toss well. Pour into a serving bowl, or spoon onto individual serving plates. Top with a sprinkling of fresh flat leaf parsley, lemon zest and a drizzle of good extra virgin olive oil. Finish with more freshly grated cheese, if desired.

GRILLED HALIBUT PROVENCAL

Recently, Jeff and I visited Alaska where we were blown away by its' incredible beauty and amazing fresh fish, wild salmon and pacific halibut in particular. Known for its very low fat content, halibut is a mild, dense and firm fish perfect for this robust, aromatic sauce. I like to serve with a simple arugula salad with a lemon vinaigrette.

2 fresh halibut filets *(at least 1-inch thick)*, **patted dry with paper towels**
3 tablespoons extra virgin olive oil
1 medium shallot, chopped
1 teaspoon garlic, minced
1 fennel bulb, halved and sliced
¼ cup flat leaf parsley, chopped
1 teaspoon fresh thyme leaves
2 teaspoons Herbs de Provence *(di-*

vided)
2 cups canned San Marzano tomatoes, diced
½ cup dry white wine
2 tablespoons capers
½ cup halved Kalamata olives
1 tablespoon lemon zest
1 tablespoon unsalted butter
2 tablespoons fresh basil, julienne

Prepare grill (or grill pan) to medium high heat. Brush fish with olive oil and generously season with course sea salt, ground pepper and Herbs de Provence. Grill 5 minutes per side, remove to plate and cover tightly with foil. Meanwhile, heat 2 tablespoons olive oil in a medium sauté pan over medium high heat. Add fennel and sauté until it is just beginning to brown. Reduce heat to medium, add shallot and thyme, continuing to cook until soft, about 5 minutes. Stir in garlic and cook for 1 minute more. Add white wine, tomato, salt, pepper, and 1 teaspoon Herbs de Provence. Simmer for 20-25 minutes until sauce has reduced and thickened. Stir in parsley, olives and capers. Add butter and stir until completely melted. Place halibut in the sauce, along with any juices left on the plate, and simmer for 3-5 minutes. Spoon some of the sauce onto a serving platter or individual serving plates. Place fish on top and spoon remaining sauce over the fish. Finish with basil and drizzle with extra virgin olive oil.

simple lemon vinaigrette

Whisk together ½ cup extra virgin olive oil, ¼ cup fresh lemon juice, ½ teaspoon kosher salt and ¼ teaspoon ground pepper. Toss vinaigrette with fresh arugula. Season to taste with more salt and pepper if desired.

TROPICAL MANGO MAHI

The sweetness of this fresh mango and avocado salsa over flaky, mild and juicy grilled Mahi is succulent and delightful. Served with coconut basmati rice, this light and flavorful dish is as pleasing to the palate as it is brilliantly colored.

2-4 fresh Mahi filets
¼ cup extra virgin olive oil
1 tablespoon Herbs de Provence

Course sea salt and freshly ground pepper to taste

Rinse Mahi filets with cold water and dry completely with paper towels. Brush all sides with extra virgin olive oil and season with herbs, salt and pepper. Heat grill (or grill pan) to medium high heat and sear fish on all sides. Move the fish to upper rack (or a side of grill without flame) and close the lid. If using a grill pan, cover loosely with foil and bring heat down to medium low. Allow the fish to steam through until desired temperature, 5-7 minutes for medium, 7-10 minutes for a dryer more flaky fish.

mango salsa

1 large fresh mango, cut into ½ inch cubes
1 medium Hass avocado, cut into ½ inch cubes
2 tablespoons fresh flat leaf parsley, chopped
1 cup cherry or grape tomatoes, quartered
1 small shallot, finely diced

¼ cup extra virgin olive oil
1 tablespoon fresh lemon juice
1 teaspoon lemon zest
1 teaspoon lime zest

Cut mango with mango splitter, which is an every-kitchen-must-have item. (OXO makes a great one!) Discard the center seed portion and cut mango into ½ inch cubes. In a small bowl combine the mango and avocado cubes, tomatoes and shallot, stirring gently. In a separate small bowl or 2-cup glass liquid measuring cup (Pyrex), whisk together olive oil and lemon juice. Add the parsley, lime and lemon zests, salt and pepper and stir to combine. Pour over the mango mixture and toss gently. Spoon salsa over and around the fish.

coconut rice

1 cup white basmati rice
½ cup coconut water
1 teaspoon lemon zest
1 tablespoon unsalted butter or extra virgin olive oil

1 tablespoon fresh flat leaf parsley, finely chopped
2 tablespoons coconut *(optional, adds more sweetness and coconut flavor)*

Combine rice and coconut water in a medium saucepan. Bring to a boil, stirring occasionally. Cover and simmer until all of the coconut water is absorbed, 18-20 minutes. Stir in remaining ingredients and season to taste with salt and pepper.

GRILLED CITRUS SALMON

I could eat salmon 7 days a week and I'm always finding new, creative ways to serve it. This one is sweet and tangy and full of flavor. Serve it with a simple spinach salad and you have a complete, delicious and healthy meal in no time flat! The salmon can be prepared on the grill (charcoal or gas), a sauté or grill pan, or under the broiler.

2 six ounce salmon filets

1 tablespoon extra virgin olive oil

½-1 tablespoon kosher salt *(or course sea salt- I like pink Himalayan for pink fish!)*

1 teaspoon fresh course ground pepper

2 tablespoons flat leaf parsley, chopped

1 teaspoon dried oregano

Glaze *(recipe below)*

Brush salmon with olive oil and season with course salt and freshly ground pepper. Spray pan or grill rack with non-stick spray. Heat the grill or pan to medium high heat (until hot) and place fish flesh side down in the pan or on the grill. Cook until fish is nicely browned or charred and turn over to skin side down. Reduce heat to medium low and brush glaze over flesh side of salmon. If you are using a charcoal grill, place coals on one side of the grill and after turning, place salmon skin side down on the side away from the coals. Cover loosely with foil and allow the fish to steam through 5-7 minutes for medium rare 8-10 minutes for medium. Brush with glaze a time or two while it continues to cook. Remove salmon with a fish spatula to individual serving plates. Finish with fresh flat leaf parsley. To broil the fish simply place salmon skin side down on the broiler pan. Brush with glaze and season with salt and pepper. Broil on high until the fish is nicely browned, turn the heat off and close the oven door until the fish is cooked through, approximately 5 minutes for medium rare, 8 minutes for medium. After the salmon has cooked to desired temperature, you can easily remove the skin by taking a knife along the edge of the fish and between the flesh and skin. Loosen the skin with a knife and use a fish spatula to easily remove the flesh of the salmon and place on serving plates. Finish by topping the salmon with a fresh sprinkle of flat leaf parsley.

the glaze

½ cup unsalted butter

½ cup good orange marmalade

1 tablespoon fresh rosemary leaves, finely chopped

1 teaspoon fresh thyme leaves

1 tablespoon flat leaf parsley, finely chopped

1 tablespoon organic honey

1 teaspoon fresh orange zest

Pinch of red pepper flakes

In a small saucepan, melt butter and marmalade together, over medium low heat, stirring until well combined. Add rosemary, parsley, and thyme, then, honey, orange zest, and red pepper. Continue to stir until the glaze is well combined and bubbles slightly. Brush glaze over flesh side of salmon several times while it cooks.

serves 2

THAI SEARED TUNA WITH COCONUT RICE

This healthy Thai inspired dish will delight the senses with its combination of flavors. The rice adds a sweet compliment to balance the cilantro soy sauce on the fish. I serve this dish with fresh sliced avocado and a side of batayaki *(see my Spinach-Shiitake Batayaki recipe, page 154).*

2 fresh Ahi tuna filets

1 tablespoon extra virgin olive oil

1 medium shallot, thinly sliced in small rings

½ cup dry white wine

1 tablespoon soy sauce *(low sodium)*

1 teaspoon fresh ginger *(grated)*

1 tablespoon unsalted butter

1-2 tablespoons fresh cilantro, chopped

1 teaspoon lime zest

Course sea salt and fresh ground pepper

Season tuna filets generously with course sea salt and fresh ground pepper. Place 1 tablespoon olive oil in sauté pan and heat on medium high until it begins to smoke. Sear fish on both sides and cook until desired temperature 1-2 minutes per side for medium rare. Remove fish from sauté pan and place it on a plate or board to rest. Cover with foil. To the sauté pan, add the shallot and stir until it begins to caramelize. Deglaze the pan with white wine and stir to reduce by half. Stir in soy sauce, ginger, lime zest, then, add butter and stir until it has melted completely. Add cilantro and turn off the heat. Slice tuna filets into 1-inch strips and place on serving plates with rice. Pour sauce over the fish and serve.

the rice

1 cup basmati rice *(White or Brown)*

½ cup coconut water

¼ cup thinly sliced almonds, lightly toasted

1 tablespoon toasted sesame seeds

1 tablespoon fresh cilantro or Thai basil, finely chopped

½ cup dried currants or white raisins

1 tablespoon scallions, thinly sliced into rings *(only the green part)*

1 teaspoon lime zest

1 tablespoon unsalted butter or extra virgin olive oil

2 tablespoons coconut *(optional, adds more sweetness and coconut flavor)*

serves 2

Prepare the rice: Place sesame seeds and almonds on a sheet of foil and lightly toast under the broiler or toss in a hot sauté pan. In a medium saucepan, bring rice and coconut water to a boil. Stir in a pinch of kosher salt and cover and simmer until all of the liquid is absorbed, 18-20 minutes. Remove from heat, add butter and stir until melted. Gently stir in remaining ingredients and season with salt and pepper to taste. Cover to keep warm until ready to plate.

Assemble: Place generous portion of rice on each of two individual serving plates. Arrange slices of tuna on serving plates with the rice. Spoon sauce over tuna and garnish with avocado slices and fresh ginger on the side.

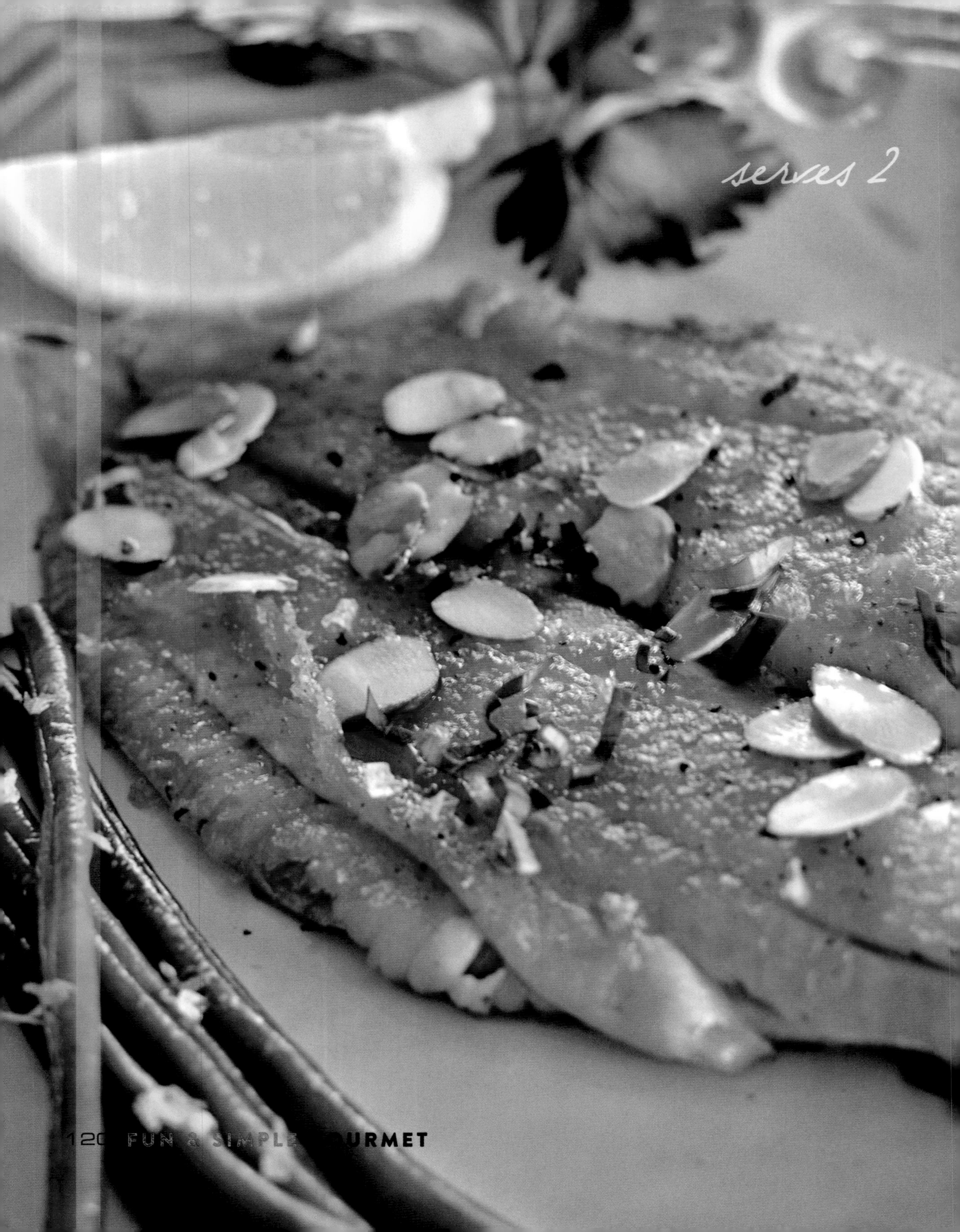

serves 2

MOUNTAIN TROUT AMANDINE

Colorado River rainbow trout are plentiful during the summer months while we are in the Rockies and one of our favorite fish. The filets are thin and mild and cook very quickly, brown and crispy on the outside, mild and juicy on the inside. I serve with a tangy lemon amandine sauce with crunchy toasted almonds.

2 large fresh trout filets (*rainbow or brook trout*)
1 tablespoon olive oil
Juice and zest of one lemon
½ cup dry white wine
1 tablespoon unsalted butter

1 tablespoon fresh flat leaf parsley, chopped
2 tablespoons sliced almonds, toasted
Course sea salt and freshly ground pepper to taste
Lemon wedges for serving

Season fish with course sea salt and ground pepper. Bring a sauté or frying pan, with 1 tablespoon olive oil, to medium high heat. When it just begins to smoke, it is ready for the fish. Sear filets, flesh side down until nicely browned, 3-5 minutes. Turn fish skin side down and reduce heat to medium, allowing fish to cook through, 3-5 minutes. Remove to plate and cover loosely with foil. Prepare sauce in same pan. Do not rinse the pan, as you want the flavors from the fish incorporated into the sauce.

lemon amandine sauce

Deglaze the pan with white wine over medium high heat scraping the browned bits from the bottom of the pan. Add the lemon juice, lemon zest and continue to stir until the liquid has reduced in half. Remove from heat, add butter and swirl until completely melted into the sauce. Toss in parsley and almonds and allow them to heat through in the sauce.

Place fish on individual serving plates. Spoon sauce over fish and serve. I like to serve with haricot verts (*steamed French-cut green beans*), lemon wedges and a crisp dry white wine.

WHITEFISH WITH FENNEL~ORANGE RELISH

This recipe is perfect for any thick, firm, white flaky fish. I like to use Grouper, Chilean Sea Bass, Black Cod, Alaskan Cod or Hog Fish *(Snapper)*. The fish is light and mild and the relish, vibrant and full of flavor, a dynamic combination.

4 white fish filets

1 tablespoon unsalted butter

1 tablespoon extra virgin olive oil

1 large seedless orange

1 medium fennel bulb *(save fronds for garnish)*

1 small shallot, thinly sliced

2 teaspoons capers *(non pareils)*

½ cup halved Kalamata olives

1 teaspoon flat leaf parsley, finely chopped

½ teaspoon dried oregano leaves

2 tablespoons extra virgin olive oil *(for relish)*

1 teaspoon orange zest

Course salt and fresh ground pepper

Preheat oven to 400 degrees. Slice fennel bulb in half and remove outer layer and core. Cut into 1-inch thick slices. Toss fennel and shallot in 1 tablespoon olive oil and season with salt and pepper. Roast until just tender and beginning to caramelize, 8-10 minutes. Remove from oven and cool to room temperature. Meanwhile, remove skin and pith from orange and carefully cut into segments. In a medium bowl, gently stir orange slices, capers, olives, parsley, oregano, and fennel mixture in 2 tablespoons extra virgin olive oil.

Reduce heat in oven to 350 degrees. Rinse and thoroughly dry fish with paper towels. Season generously with course sea salt and ground pepper. Spray an oven resistant sauté pan with non-stick spray and add 1 tablespoon each olive oil and unsalted butter. Heat over medium high heat until pan is hot and butter begins to foam but not burn. Cook fish on both sides until beautifully golden brown, turning only once. Place pan in the oven until the fish is cooked through, 3-5 minutes, depending on its thickness. Place fish on a serving platter or individual serving plates and spoon relish over fish. Finish with a sprinkling of finely chopped flat leaf parsley and orange zest. Season with salt and ground pepper to taste and a drizzle of extra virgin olive oil. Garnish with fennel fronds.

serves 4

WHOLE ROASTED SNAPPER

Jeff's favorite fish is a whole roasted snapper prepared on the grill. We are so fortunate that we have access to fresh caught snapper almost anytime. When shopping for a whole snapper, on the bone, it is easy to determine if it is fresh by the clarity of the eyes. Jeff loves for us to serve it on a big platter in the middle of the table, that way everyone just dives in. The skin is so crispy and delicious, the meat juicy and mild. Have your Fish Monger scale the fish and clean its cavity so that it is ready for you to prepare.

5-6 pound whole snapper
¼ cup extra virgin olive oil
1 small shallot, thinly sliced
1 lemon, thinly sliced
1 lime, thinly sliced
1 tablespoon dried oregano
1 tablespoon course sea salt and fresh ground pepper *(or to taste)*

Prepare grill by spraying rack with non-stick spray and heat to the highest setting. Rinse fish and dry thoroughly with paper towels. Season cavity with salt, pepper and oregano and lay slices of shallot, lemon and lime inside. Brush skin generously with olive oil and season generously with course sea salt and ground pepper. Score the skin on both sides of the fish with 3 or 4 slits, depending on the size of the fish. When the grill is hot, sear fish on both sides until the skin is brown and crispy and the fish is flaky and opaque, 5-7 minutes per side. Reduce heat to low and close lid allowing the fish to cook through another 5-10 minutes depending on its size.

The fish is done when a knife slides easily through the thickest part of the flesh. Transfer to a serving platter and garnish with lemon and lime wedges. Pour half of the lemon vinaigrette dressing over the fish and serve the remaining dressing along side the fish in a sauce dish. Start by digging into the top side of the fish, when the center bone appears, it can easily be removed by pulling it away from the fish (including the head). Set aside and continue with the bottom half!

the lemon vinaigrette

¾ cup extra virgin olive oil
¼ cup fresh squeezed lemon juice
1 tablespoon fresh lemon zest
1 teaspoon dried oregano

1 tablespoon scallions (green onions) chopped
Sea salt and ground pepper to taste

Whisk all ingredients together in a small bowl.

COLORADO RACK OF LAMB

There is not a dish that reminds me more of being in the Rockies, than a fresh Rack of Lamb. It is tender and succulent, and so versatile. Perfect for a barbeque or traditional holiday dinner. Mine has a hint of lemon, complimented with garlic, rosemary and thyme, perfect for the lamb. Finished with a red wine reduction...sweet, savory and so delicious.

1 **French-cut rack of lamb**
1 **tablespoon Kosher salt**
1 **tablespoon course ground pepper**
2 **garlic cloves, minced**
1 **teaspoon lemon juice**
1 **teaspoon lemon zest**

1 **tablespoon extra virgin olive oil**
2 **tablespoons rosemary leaves, finely chopped**
1 **tablespoon fresh thyme leaves**
Fresh rosemary and thyme stalks for garnish (if desired)

Place Rack of Lamb in roasting pan fat side up (ribs curving down). Season generously with kosher salt and course pepper. Make a paste with the garlic, rosemary, thyme, lemon juice, lemon zest, and olive oil. Spread evenly over the fatty side of the rack. Allow prepared rack to rest at room temperature for approximately one hour.

Preheat oven or grill to 450 degrees. Roast lamb for 20-25 minutes until internal temperature reaches 120-125 degrees for rare, 125-130 for medium rare. Remove to cutting board and allow to rest, loosely covered with foil, 10-15 minutes, reserving pan juices for the sauce. Slice rack between each rib bone and place on a serving platter. Spoon sauce over ribs and serve.

the sauce

Reserved pan drippings
1 **garlic clove, minced**
1 **teaspoon fresh thyme leaves**

½ **cup dry red wine** (or red wine vinegar)
1 **tablespoon unsalted butter**

Bring pan juices to a mild boil over medium high heat. When the juices begin to bubble, add wine, thyme and garlic, stirring to combine. Reduce heat to medium and allow the sauce to reduce slightly. Add the butter and swirl until completely melted. Spoon sauce over lamb ribs and garnish with fresh rosemary and thyme stalks if desired.

serves 2 to 4

GRILLED LAMB CHOPS
WITH KALE~MINT PESTO

These juicy chops will make your mouth water just smelling them cook! The pesto melts right into the warm lamb and adds so much fresh flavor. I like to serve with roasted new potatoes and a green vegetable and/or salad.

4 premium quality lamb chops
1 tablespoon extra virgin olive oil
½ teaspoon dried oregano
1 teaspoon fresh thyme leaves, finely chopped

1 teaspoon fresh rosemary leaves, finely chopped
Kosher salt and fresh ground pepper to taste

kale pesto

1 small garlic clove
¼-½ cup extra virgin olive oil
½ cup toasted walnuts, chopped
1 cup fresh basil leaves
1 cup kale leaves, chopped (stems removed)

¼ cup fresh mint leaves
½ cup grated Parmigiano-Reggiano cheese
Kosher salt and fresh ground pepper to taste

Pulse garlic and walnuts in food processor until nuts are well ground. Add basil, kale and mint and 1 tablespoon olive oil and process until beginning to come together. Add more oil gradually through the feeding tube until pesto is smooth. Place in a small bowl and stir in cheese and salt and pepper to taste. Set aside.

Spray grill or grill pan on stove top with non-stick spray and heat to medium high heat. Brush lamb chops with olive oil and season with salt, pepper and oregano. When cooking surface is hot add the chops and cook until meat thermometer reads 140 degrees for medium rare, 145 for medium, 3 to 4 minutes per side, turning only once. Remove to plate and sprinkle with the fresh chopped thyme and rosemary leaves. Allow to rest 5-10 minutes. Spoon 1-2 tablespoons pesto on each of two serving plates. Arrange two chops on each plate on top of pesto. With a spoon or pastry brush, spread a light coating of pesto over the top of the chops.

serves 2

FILET OF BEEF TENDERLOIN

PAN ROASTED WITH RICH RED WINE REDUCTION

Another staple in our home. Jeff likes a good steak, usually once a week, and in his mind, there is no steak except a Filet Mignon. This one is tender and juicy, a great choice for date night at home, or entertaining a small crowd for a dinner party. Tenderloin of beef should be served medium rare, though Jeff prefers his on the "medium rare-rare" side. Simply prepared, yet a richly elegant dish for any occasion.

2 eight-ounce Certified Angus Beef Tenderloin Steaks
1 tablespoon extra virgin olive oil
½ cup dry red wine
2 teaspoons unsalted butter *(divided into 2 one-teaspoon butter pats)*

1 small shallot, thinly sliced *(into rings)*
1 teaspoon fresh thyme, finely chopped
4 ounces mixed mushrooms *(cremini, shitake, oyster) See Simple Mushroom Sauté recipe, Accompaniments & Tasteful Sides.*

Bring steaks to room temperature, which will take 30 minutes to 1 hour depending on their thickness. Season well with course sea salt (or kosher salt) and course ground pepper. Heat 1 tablespoon olive oil in a large sauté pan over medium high heat. When the pan it hot, sear the steaks until browned, 3-4 minutes per side. Reduce heat to medium low and loosely cover with foil allowing steaks to cook through to desired temperature ideally medium rare, 3-5 minutes more. The internal temperature should read 125 degrees. Remove to platter and place one butter pat on each steak. Allow to rest, loosely covered with foil, 5-10 minutes while you prepare the sauce. When ready to serve, you might prefer to slice the steaks on the diagonal into ½-1-inch strips, or serve whole, just as they are.

the sauce

Bring pan to medium heat and deglaze by adding the red wine, scraping any browned bits from the bottom and sides of the sauté pan. Add shallot and thyme and stir while the wine reduces to approximately ¼ cup (in half). Turn heat off and add butter, swirling until melted and incorporated in wine reduction.

To serve, spoon a tablespoon of the sauce on each of two serving plates. Place steaks on top of sauce, and spoon remaining sauce over top and around the steaks. Finish with sautéed mushrooms.

VEAL OSSOBUCO

Another highly requested dish by my dinner guests and one of Jeff's favorite meals. Ossobuco translates, "bone with a hole" and originates in Milan, the West Lombard region of Italy. It is traditionally served with Risotto Milanese, saffron risotto, but can also be served very well with pasta or mashed potatoes. At our house, it is always true Milanese style...a Gigi specialty.

4-6 cross cut veal shanks, 2 inches thick *(by your butcher)*

¼ cup extra virgin olive oil

1 medium onion, chopped

1 medium carrot, sliced in ¼ inch rounds

1 medium celery rib, chopped into ¼ inch pieces

3 cloves garlic, minced

1 tablespoon fresh thyme leaves

1 teaspoon dried oregano

28 ounce can San Marzano tomatoes, whole

3 cups dry white wine

1-2 tablespoons fresh lemon juice

1 tablespoon lemon zest

Kosher salt and fresh ground pepper to taste

Preheat oven to 350 degrees. Season Ossobuco with salt and pepper. Heat a large roasting pan with olive oil over medium high heat. Sear veal on all sides until nicely browned, 8-10 minutes. Remove to a plate, drizzle with fresh lemon juice and set aside. Add onion, carrot and celery to the roasting pan and cook on medium heat until soft and beginning to brown stirring frequently, 5-7 minutes. Add garlic, thyme and oregano and cook for 1 minute longer. Add wine and stir, deglazing the bottom of the pan. Meanwhile, pour tomatoes and their juice into a medium bowl and smash with your hands, or a spoon. Add to the roasting pan, and season with salt and pepper. Bring to a boil. Carefully place veal into the sauce and sprinkle with lemon zest. If the veal is not immersed in the sauce at least half way, add a little chicken broth to the liquid. Cover and roast for 2½ hours, until the meat is tender and falls off the bone. Place veal on a serving platter or individual serving plates and spoon the ragu (sauce from the roasting pan) over the Ossobuco. To finish, generously sprinkle with gremolata.

gremolata

Zest of one lemon

2 tablespoons flat leaf parsley, finely chopped

¼ cup toasted pine nuts *(pinioli)*

¼ cup Parmigiano-Reggiano cheese, finely grated

Mix together all ingredients in a small bowl with your fingertips.

serves 4 to 6

VEAL PICCATA

This light, lemony and crispy veal scaloppini makes a fantastic anytime meal. So simple to prepare with very little prep and cooking time. Serve with my *lemony chevre mashed potatoes* and a side salad, or, vermicelli pasta *(very thin spaghetti)* tossed in the sauce. You will love the lemony tang and delicately light texture of this dish.

6-8 thin boneless veal cutlets
  (scaloppini)
½ cup all purpose flour
1 tablespoon extra virgin olive oil
½ cup dry white wine
2 tablespoons fresh lemon juice

1 tablespoon fresh lemon zest
1 teaspoon capers
1 tablespoon flat leaf parsley, finely chopped
Kosher salt and fresh ground pepper to taste

Place veal scaloppini between 2 sheets of wax or parchment paper on top of a cutting board. With a mallet or meat pounder, flatten the cutlets, tenderizing in the process. Heat a medium sauté pan with 1 tablespoon olive oil over medium high heat. Place flour, salt and pepper in a shallow bowl or baking dish mix well with your fingers. Dredge veal in the mixture dusting it evenly. Sauté veal until lightly browned, about one minute per side. Remove to a warm platter and cover with foil to keep warm. Add the wine to the sauté pan to deglaze, scraping any browned bits from the pan. Reduce heat to medium low and allow the sauce to reduce slightly as the alcohol cooks off. Add lemon juice, lemon zest, capers and parsley. Continue to cook over medium low heat another minute or two. Add butter and swirl into sauce.

When the butter is completely melted, pour the sauce over the veal and serve immediately. Garnish with slices of lemon. Season with more salt and pepper to taste if desired.

vermicelli

If serving with vermicelli, cook ½ pound of the pasta according to package directions while you are sautéing the veal. When the sauce is finished, bring the pasta from the pasta water with tongs or a pasta spoon directly into the sauté pan and toss in the sauce. Add 2 additional tablespoons of unsalted butter and stir until melted. Spoon pasta onto a serving platter or individual serving plates and top with freshly grated Parmigiano-Reggiano cheese. Place the veal cutlets directly on top of the vermicelli and pour, or spoon, the remaining sauce from the sauté pan over the veal. Finish with a sprinkling of finely chopped flat leaf parsley.

serves 2 to 4

EASY ROASTED CHICKEN

Perfect for a family Sunday dinner, or any day. The aroma of a roasting chicken with fresh herbs and white wine, will make your family feel like it is a holiday any day of the week. Serve with my simple *lemony caesar salad* and a crispy baguette for a simple and casual meal, or with white wine gravy, mashed potatoes and haricots verts amandine for a more elaborate dinner. This recipe is also wonderful for roasting a perfect turkey.

1 largewhole chicken, 5-8 pounds
2 medium lemons, cut into wedges
  (plus a few more wedges for serving)
1 head garlic, halved
½ cup organic chicken stock or broth
½ cup dry white wine
1 tablespoon Herbs de Provence

1 tablespoon Kosher salt
½ tablespoon freshly ground pepper
1 bouquet garni of fresh herbs,
  (one bunch each, fresh rosemary and thyme stalks, sage leaves, bay leaf, and flat leaf parsley tied together with kitchen string.)

Preheat oven to 450 degrees. Thoroughly rinse chicken and pat dry with paper towels inside and out. Place chicken in shallow roasting pan breast side up. Season cavity with salt and pepper and stuff with bouquet garni of fresh herbs and the garlic halves. Squeeze lemon wedges inside the cavity and rub on the skin, then, place inside the cavity along with the herbs for roasting. Pour stock and wine around the chicken in the roasting pan. Generously rub extra virgin olive oil on skin and season well with course salt and pepper. Sprinkle with Herbs de Provence. Reduce oven temperature to 350 degrees and roast 1 to 1½ hours, until internal temperature reaches 160-165 degrees. Remove from the oven and cover tightly with foil. Allow the chicken to rest 20 minutes before carving. Move chicken to cutting board and carve by first removing wings, then, leg quarters (legs/thighs), set aside. Taking your knife along either side of the breast bone, remove each breast and cut crosswise into 1-inch slices. Arrange slices on a serving platter and spoon some of the au jus from the pan drippings over the meat. Add wings, legs and thighs to the platter and garnish with fresh rosemary springs.

white wine gravy

Pour pan drippings through mesh sieve or strainer into a sauté pan after removing the chicken to a cutting board. Prepare roux by whisking 2 tablespoons of flour into ½ cup warm tap water. Season roux with 1 teaspoon salt and ½ teaspoon pepper and set aside. Bring pan drippings to a boil and reduce heat to medium. Whisk in the roux until thickened. Remove from heat and add white wine in ½ cup increments, whisking thoroughly after each addition, until desired consistency is reached. Season to taste with more salt and pepper if needed.

GINGER GLAZED CHICKEN

Spice up a plain grilled chicken breast with this mouth watering, fragrant and gingery glaze. Served with grilled baby bok choy—a fresh and fabulous combination of flavors and aromatics.

4-6 skin-on free range chicken breasts
1 cup ginger preserves
½ cup (1 stick) unsalted butter
¼ cup organic honey

1 tablespoon Herbs de Provence
1 tablespoon fresh orange zest
1 teaspoon freshly grated ginger
1 cup fresh cilantro, rough chop

In a small saucepan over medium heat, melt butter together with ginger preserves. Stir until well combined. Add honey, herbs, zest, ginger and cilantro and stir until honey has melted into the sauce. Set aside. Preheat grill to medium high. Pat chicken breasts dry with paper towels and season well with salt and pepper. Turn one side of the grill off and place the chicken skin side down over the indirect heat. Cook for 10 minutes and turn to skin side up. With basting brush, coat chicken well with glaze and cook for 10 minutes more. Again, turn the chicken over, baste and cook for 10 minutes, then one final turn to skin side up, baste and cook 10 minutes more, 40-45 minutes total, or until the internal temperature of the chicken is at least 160 degrees. Allow to rest, covered loosely with foil, 5-10 minutes before serving.

the baby bok choy

2-4 heads baby bok choy, split length wise, rinsed and dried
½ cup extra virgin olive oil
¼ cup fresh squeezed lemon juice

1 tablespoon soy sauce
1 teaspoon kosher salt
½ teaspoon ground pepper
1/8 teaspoon crushed red pepper

In a medium bowl, whisk together olive oil, lemon, soy sauce, salt and peppers. Add baby bok choy and toss to coat with the dressing. While the chicken is resting, place bok choy cut side down on hot side of grill until charred, approximately 1 minute. Turn and cook 1 minute longer. Turn heat off and move bok choy to upper rack of grill, away from heat. Close lid and cook until tender, about 3-5 minutes. Serve immediately alongside chicken.

serves 4 to 6

ROASTED GAME HEN
WITH LEMON, ROSEMARY AND THYME

serves 2 to 4

My husband Jeff can't live without a roasted hen at least once a week. These little guys are so simple to prepare and always a crowd pleaser. Fresh free-range hens are fantastic, but Tyson's Cornish Game Hens in the freezer section are very good if you can't find fresh. Add a few new potatoes to the roasting pan, and you have a one pot meal. I generally serve with my *lemony caesar salad.*

2 whole Cornish game hens	½ cup dry white wine
1 lemon, quartered	½ teaspoon Herbs de Provence
4 sprigs fresh rosemary	Course sea salt or Kosher salt
10-20 sprigs fresh thyme	Freshly ground black pepper
4 cloves garlic, smashed and peeled	10-15 small new potatoes *(optional)*

Preheat oven to 375 degrees. Drizzle roasting pan with extra virgin olive oil to coat the bottom of the pan. I prefer a cast iron roasting pan, but any roaster will do. Rinse hens thoroughly and pat them dry. Trim excess fat/skin and squeeze the juice from ¼ lemon inside each cavity leaving the lemon quarter inside. Stuff each hen with 2 sprigs of rosemary, 5-10 sprigs of thyme and 2 garlic cloves. Place in a roasting pan breast side up and squeeze the remaining lemon over hens. Generously drizzle with good extra virgin olive oil. Rub skin to coat evenly and season with course salt and ground black pepper. Sprinkle each hen with ½ teaspoon thyme leaves and ¼ teaspoon Herbs de Provence. Pour white wine around hens in the bottom of the roasting pan.

Roast uncovered 45 minutes to one hour until meat thermometer reads 165 degrees and skin is golden brown. After 30 minutes, new potatoes can be added to roasting pan around hens to cook in the pan juices, soaking up this wonderful flavor. Make sure the potatoes are at room temperature when you add them to the roasting pan (not cold from the refrigerator).

Remove from oven and loosely cover with foil to rest 10 minutes. To serve, bring hens to a board and cut along the breast bone length wise on both sides, pulling breast meat away from bone. Remove herb stuffing. Carefully remove spine and tail bone from each half with a sharp knife and arrange hens on a serving platter or individual plates. Spoon pan juices over hens and serve with roasted new potatoes or mashed potatoes. Garnish serving platter with a few sprigs of rosemary, thyme and lemon wedges.

Accompaniments
& TASTEFUL SIDES

Just as who you spend time with enhances any occasion, what you serve with a main dish complements the meal and enhances flavor.

Finding accompaniments that enrich character and taste and look appetizing on a plate, will refine any meal with very little effort.

Simple to spectacular!

Accompaniments

& TASTEFUL SIDES

ARUGULA SALAD

My favorite accompaniment to a rich and heavy main dish. The arugula is peppery and fresh, and the dressing light and lemony. Topped with shaved Parmigiano Reggiano cheese, perfectly simple. You will see this side salad recommended to serve with my Veal Ossobuco as well as many other hearty main dishes.

1 large package baby arugula

½ cup extra virgin olive oil *(first cold pressed)*

2 tablespoons freshly squeezed lemon juice

1 teaspoon lemon zest

Course sea salt *(or kosher salt)* and freshly ground pepper to taste

Shaved Parmigiano Reggiano cheese

Rinse arugula thoroughly and dry well in paper towels. Place in a large bowl. In a small bowl, whisk together the olive oil, lemon juice and lemon zest. Pour over arugula leaves and toss well. Spoon onto a serving platter and season generously with course salt and pepper.

With a cheese shaver or vegetable peeler, shave strips of Parmigiano Reggiano over top and serve. For a hint of decadence, finish with a scant drizzle of white truffle oil. *(optional)*

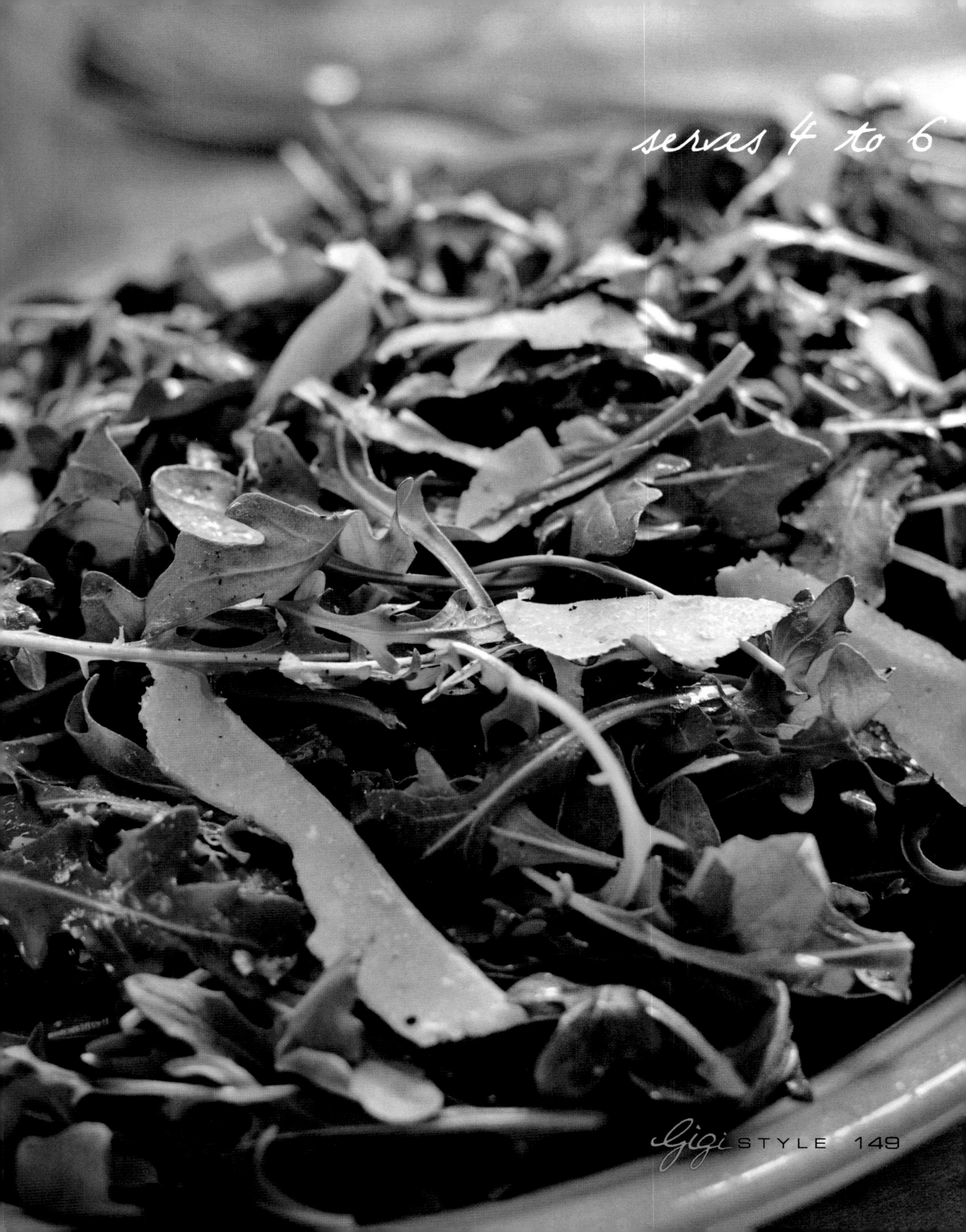

serves 4 to 6

ROASTED ASPARAGUS

serves 4 to 6

What I love about roasting vegetables is that they retain their beautiful color and flavor. Not to mention it is so effortless. Asparagus is a great vegetable for roasting, the exterior is a bit crispy and caramelizes with the olive oil. The inside, tender, juicy and flavorful. The sea salt enhances the flavor of the asparagus and brings out its sweetness. Jeff isn't a vegetable fan, but he thinks this one tastes like candy!

1 large bunch medium asparagus
2 tablespoons extra virgin olive oil

Course sea salt and fresh ground pepper to taste
Fresh lemon zest *(for serving)*

Preheat oven to 400 degrees. Rinse and thoroughly dry asparagus on paper towels and trim the dried ends from the bottom. Place in a shallow 3-4 quart oblong baking dish. A LeCreuset 3½ quart oval baking dish is perfect. Toss with olive oil, salt and pepper.

Roast until tender and crispy, 15-20 minutes depending on the size of the stalks. Test with a fork after 10 minutes for desired tenderness. Remove immediately from the baking dish onto a serving platter as the asparagus will continue to cook in the hot baking dish even after you remove from the oven. Drizzle with a little more extra virgin olive oil and finish with fresh lemon zest. Season to taste with more course salt and pepper.

That's it! So simple and a great side vegetable with almost any dish.

HEIRLOOM TOMATO SALAD

This one is all about the colorful heirloom tomatoes. Flaky Cypress sea salt and a light, simple sherry vinaigrette, enhance the flavor of the ripe tomatoes and make them shine as the star of this beautiful salad. A super appetizer salad or side salad with any dish.

1 quart heirloom tomatoes (assorted colors)
8 oz. baby spinach leaves
8 oz. romaine lettuce

¼ cup pine nuts (toasted)
Flaky sea salt to taste (Cypress or Maldon)
Fresh ground pepper to taste

Rinse romaine and spinach and dry thoroughly. Cut romaine stalks horizontally into strips that match the size of the baby spinach leaves. Arrange lettuce and spinach on a chilled serving platter or individual serving plates. Quarter larger tomatoes into wedges, slicing the smaller tomatoes in half and place in a medium bowl. Pour half of the dressing over the tomatoes and gently stir to coat the tomatoes. Spoon over lettuce and spinach and top with the toasted pine nuts.

Drizzle some (or all) of the remaining dressing over the salad and finish with a generous sprinkle of toasted pine nuts, flaky sea salt and freshly ground black pepper to taste.

sherry vinaigrette

½ cup extra virgin olive oil
1 tablespoon sherry wine vinegar
1 tablespoon shallot, finely chopped

Dash of flaky sea salt (Cypress or Maldon)
Fresh ground pepper to taste

In a small bowl, whisk together the olive oil and vinegar until emulsified. Add shallot, salt and pepper and stir until well combined.

SPINACH~SHIITAKE BATAYAKI

The most delicious and beautiful way I know to serve sautéed spinach. Although Asian inspired, this side will compliment any main dish, meat, fish or poultry and of course, it is perfect with sushi or sashimi.

1 large garlic clove, thinly sliced

1 teaspoons shallot, thinly sliced

1 teaspoon red pepper flakes, or to taste

2 tablespoons extra virgin olive oil

4 cups shiitake mushrooms, thinly sliced

4 cups baby spinach leaves

2 tablespoons fresh chives, finely chopped

Course sea salt and freshly ground pepper to taste

1 tablespoon toasted sesame seeds *(optional)*

Warm olive oil in a large sauté pan over medium heat. Add shallot, mushrooms and red pepper, allowing to sweat and begin to caramelize 6-8 minutes. Add garlic and stir. Add spinach and toss well. Cook, stirring occasionally until spinach is wilted and still bright green, 5-7 minutes.

Spoon onto serving platter or bowl and season with course sea salt and pepper to taste. Finish with freshly chopped chives and toasted sesame seeds if desired.

serves 4 to 6

GRILLED BABY BOK CHOY

Bok Choy is a wonderful, healthy side vegetable, especially grilled. You will love the combination of the charred flavor from the grill and spicy soy dressing.

2-4 heads baby Bok Choy, split lengthwise, rinsed and dried

½ cup extra virgin olive oil

¼ cup fresh squeezed lemon juice

1 tablespoon soy sauce

1 teaspoon kosher salt

½ teaspoon ground pepper

⅛ teaspoon crushed red pepper

In a medium bowl, whisk together olive oil, lemon, soy sauce, salt and peppers. Add baby Bok Choy and toss to coat in the dressing. Place Bok Choy cut side down on the hot side of the grill until charred, approximately 1 minute. Turn and cook for 1 minute longer. Then, turn heat off and move Bok Choy to the upper rack of grill, away from the heat. If grilling with charcoal, leave one side of the grill without coals, then simply move the Bok Choy to the side of the grill away from the coals.

Close the lid of the grill and cook until tender, 3-5 minutes. Remove from grill and brush one more time with the dressing prior to serving. Season again with more salt and pepper to taste if desired.

serves 2 to 4

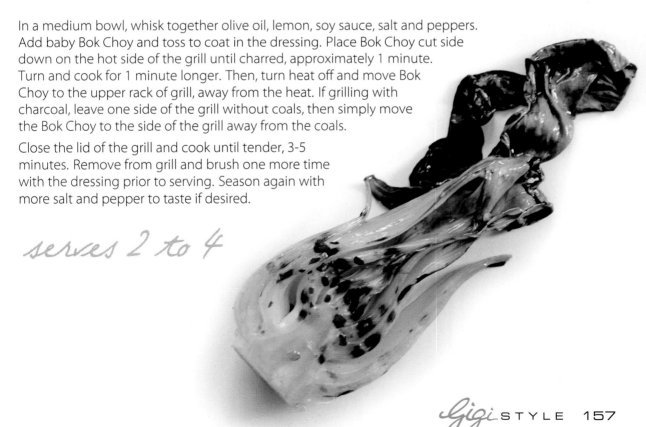

HARICOTS VERTS AMANDINE
serves 4 to 6

A simply elegant vegetable side with any meal, I serve Haricots Verts with everything from steaks on the grill to an elegant holiday feast. I like to prepare the beans ahead of time so that they are perfectly cooked, then just reheat in butter at serving time.

1 lb. fresh French cut green beans
1 tablespoon lemon zest, grated
¼ cup shaved almonds, toasted
¼ cup *(½ stick)* unsalted butter

1 teaspoon kosher salt, plus a pinch before serving
Ground pepper to taste

Prepare an ice bath with cold water and ice cubes in a medium bowl. Bring 1 quart of water and 1 teaspoon kosher salt to a boil. Add green beans and boil until bright green and al dente consistency, not raw, but still firm, 3-5 minutes. Test with a fork or taste. Using tongs or a spider, move beans into the ice bath to stop cooking. This will also help them to retain their beautiful bright green color. When the beans have cooled, transfer to paper towels and dry completely. Cover with plastic wrap, or place in a Ziploc bag and refrigerate until you are ready to re-heat. Remove from refrigerator 20 minutes prior to re-heating to bring to room temperature.

Melt butter in medium sauté pan on medium heat until it begins to foam. Turn off heat and add beans to sauté pan, stirring into the butter until heated through. Pour into a serving dish and top with grated lemon zest, kosher salt and pepper to taste. Finish with toasted almonds.

LEMONY CHEVRE MASHED POTATOES

You will love the creamy texture and hint of lemon in these decadent mashed potatoes, my favorite side dish with Grilled Lobster Tails and Colorado Rack of Lamb. You will also see this recipe in my Lobster Martini Appetizer. *(Appetizers, Soups & Small Plates)*. The beauty of this side is that these fluffy potatoes can be prepared in advance and simply re-heated at serving time. Perfect for a dinner party or holiday meal.

4 large baking potatoes
¼ cup (½ stick) unsalted butter
1 cup organic chicken broth
½ to 1 cup warm milk *(any fat content)*
4 oz. lemon Chevre goat cheese

1 tablespoon fresh lemon zest
1 tablespoon flat leaf parsley or fresh chives, finely chopped
Kosher salt and course ground pepper to taste

Pierce potatoes with a fork and bake in a 400 degree oven until soft, 45 minutes to 1 hour. They can also be baked in the microwave oven. While potatoes are baking, bring Chevre to room temperature on the kitchen counter. When potatoes are soft, remove from oven with oven mitt and slice in half lengthwise. With a large spoon, scoop potato out of each half into a large mixing bowl while they are still hot. Add ¼ cup unsalted butter and the Chevre. Mash with potato masher until well combined. Then, using an electric mixer, begin whipping potatoes on low speed adding ¼ cup of the broth at a time, slowly increasing speed until all of the broth has been absorbed into the potatoes. Add warm milk ¼ cup at a time until desired consistency is reached. Finish with lemon zest, salt and pepper, and whip on high speed until fluffy. Serve immediately. If preparing in advance, add a few butter pats on top and bring to room temperature prior to re-heating in the microwave. Stir well and serve topped with freshly chopped chives or flat leaf parsley and serve immediately.

regular mashed potatoes

4-6 large Yukon baking potatoes
1-2 cups organic chicken or vegetable broth

½ cup unsalted butter
Kosher salt and freshly ground pepper to taste

After potatoes have been scooped into bowl, add butter and mash until well combined. Using an electric mixer, begin whipping on low speed adding broth slowly, ¼ cup at a time, then increasing speed until desired consistency is reached. Season with salt and pepper.

MEDITERRANEAN POTATO SALAD

This fresh potato salad is colorful and flavorful, alongside my *Steak Victor* or grilled lamb chops, for a perfect and deliciously different barbeque. Serve with toasted or grilled pita brushed with extra virgin olive oil and a sprinkling of sea salt and dried oregano.

24 new potatoes *(white, red or combination)*
12 grape tomatoes, halved
½ cup halved Kalamata olives
2 Hass avocados, cut into 1 inch cubes
1 cup baby spinach leaves
1 teaspoon capers

¼ cup fresh mint leaves, torn
1 cup scallions (green onions) finely chopped
¼ cup fresh basil, julienne
Course sea salt and freshly ground pepper to taste

Boil potatoes in a pot of rapidly boiling salted water until tender but still firm. Remove from water and place in a medium bowl. Cut each potato in half lengthwise and toss with ⅓ of the dressing while they are still warm, set aside. As the potatoes rest they will absorb the dressing and its flavors. When they reach room temperature, add the tomatoes, olives, spinach, mint, scallions and half of the remaining dressing. Toss well. Pour into a serving bowl, and gently stir in the avocado. Season to taste with salt and pepper and drizzle remaining dressing over top. Finish with julienne of fresh basil.

the dressing

¾ cup extra virgin olive oil
¼ cup sherry vinegar
1 tablespoon mint leaves finely chopped
1 tablespoon fresh basil leaves finely chopped

1 small shallot, minced
1 tablespoon fresh lemon zest
1 teaspoon fresh lemon juice
1 teaspoon Herbs de Provence
Course sea salt and freshly ground pepper to taste

In a small bowl, whisk together olive oil, vinegar and lemon juice until emulsified. Add remaining ingredients and whisk until well combined. Season to taste with sea salt and pepper.

serves 6 to 8

serves 4 to 6

ROASTED NEW POTATOES

These savory potatoes are roasted with fresh herbs, so simple, so delicious. Roasting potatoes rather than boiling, intensifies their flavor and gives their skin a crispy crust. A perfect potato side to nearly every dish and with any meal. They are fantastic breakfast potatoes, a flavorful addition on a mixed green salad or Tuna Nicoise and they make an extraordinary potato salad.

2 pounds new potatoes

2 tablespoons extra virgin olive oil

1 tablespoon rosemary leaves, finely chopped

1 tablespoon fresh thyme leaves

1 teaspoon dried oregano

Course sea salt and freshly ground pepper to taste

Preheat oven to 400 degrees. Rinse potatoes and dry thoroughly with paper towels. In a medium bowl, toss potatoes with olive oil, thyme, rosemary, oregano, salt and pepper until they are evenly coated with all of the ingredients. Pour onto a baking sheet or low-rimmed roasting pan. Roast until potatoes are brown and crispy on the outside and tender on the inside, 15-20 minutes depending on the size of the potatoes.

ROASTED WINTER VEGETABLES

As these savory winter vegetables roast, their natural sugars caramelize, giving an amazing nutty flavor and brown, caramel, color. Tender but firm, with seasoned aromatics, a divine winter side dish, a beautiful accompaniment to a holiday or special occasion, yet simple enough to prepare with any meal any day of the week.

1 bunch baby carrots, peeled and halved lengthwise

1 medium shallot, sliced

1 medium parsnip

1 pound New potatoes, quartered lengthwise *(into small wedges)*

1 pound Brussel sprouts, rinsed and halved

¼ cup extra virgin olive oil

1 teaspoon fresh thyme leaves, roughly chopped

1 teaspoon dried Herbs de Provence

Course sea salt *(or kosher salt)* and fresh ground pepper to taste

Preheat oven to 425 degrees and prepare vegetables. Line a sheet pan with aluminum foil and arrange vegetables on pan. Drizzle with olive oil and season with herbs, salt and pepper. Roast vegetables until tender and just beginning to brown and caramelize, 15-20 minutes.

Vegetables can be prepared in advance and kept at room temperature for up to 3 hours. Then simply reheated on a sheet pan. Remove vegetables to serving platter and garnish with bunches of fresh thyme if desired.

SIMPLE SAUTÉED MUSHROOMS

This simple side dish of caramelized mushrooms is a beautiful and savory compliment for almost any dish. I use these mushrooms in everything from omlettes, to kushiyaki and alongside veal and beef. They are absolutely magnificent on a holiday table. My favorite mushrooms are Shiitake and Cremini, but any combination of mushrooms that you like are just fine.

2 tablespoons extra virgin olive oil

4 oz. mixed mushrooms *(Cremini, Shiitake, Oyster)* sliced

1 teaspoon fresh thyme leaves, plus more for serving

1 garlic clove, finely minced *(optional)*

1 tablespoon unsalted butter

1 teaspoon fresh chives, finely chopped

Course sea salt or kosher salt and freshly ground pepper to taste

Bring a small sauté pan with olive oil to medium heat. Add mushrooms, stirring well to coat. Add thyme and season with salt and pepper. Sauté until the mushrooms are brown and caramelized, about 5 minutes. Add garlic if desired and stir. Cook one minute and remove from heat. For added richness and decadence, stir in one tablespoon unsalted butter until completely melted. Transfer to a serving bowl and season with more salt and pepper to taste and a sprinkling of finely chopped chives and thyme leaves.

serves 4 to 6

something

Dessert…the grand finale of every meal! Perhaps this is where the saying, "always save the best for last," comes from. Your guests will be left with a memorable and lasting impression ~

Just a bite of a something sweet to make everything seem complete!

sweet

DESERVED
DESSERTS

BASIC CITRUS CHEESECAKE

Who can go wrong with an amazing cheesecake for dessert. I had my first slice at Sardis in New York when I was a little girl. I thought it was the best thing I had ever tasted. This one is rich, yet light. Top it any way you like. I offer a few suggestions.

the crust

1 cup graham cracker crumbs

½ cup organic light brown sugar

½ cup toasted pine nuts

½ cup unsalted butter, melted

the filling

5 eight-ounce packages organic light cream cheese (room temperature)

1½ cups organic cane sugar

5 organic eggs

2 organic egg yolks

1 teaspoon Madagascar vanilla extract

1 teaspoon freshly squeezed lemon juice

1 tablespoon freshly grated zest of lemon

1 teaspoon freshly grated zest of orange

Preheat oven to 350 degrees. Place pine nuts on a sheet of aluminum foil and toast in the oven until golden brown, 5-8 minutes. Let them cool and grind in food processor or spice grinder until fine. Combine in a medium bowl with the remaining crust ingredients and press into a spring form pan on the bottom and up all sides. Bake crust until lightly browned and set, 8-10 minutes. Cool completely on a wire rack. Raise oven temperature to 450 degrees. Cream cheese and sugar until light and fluffy with a stand mixer, using the paddle attachment (or electric mixer). Add eggs and yolks, one at a time, mixing well with each addition. Scrape sides and bottom of bowl with spatula. Add remaining ingredients and stir on low speed until just blended. Pour into prepared crust.

Bake 15 minutes then reduce heat to 250 degrees and bake for 1 hour. Turn the oven off, open the oven door and let cake continue to cook approximately 20 minutes longer until center has set. Cool on a wire rack to room temperature, then refrigerate at least 8 hours or overnight. Remove cake from spring form pan onto a serving platter. Allow the cake to come to room temperature before serving. When slicing, dip your knife into a tall glass of warm water and wipe with a towel in between each slice.

Spoon a dollop of freshly whipped mascarpone cream over each slice topped with a dash of lemon and/or orange zest and serve.

mascarpone cream

1 cup chilled heavy cream *(organic)*

½ cup Mascarpone cheese
(or cream cheese)

¼ cup organic cane sugar

1 teaspoon good vanilla extract
(Madagascar bourbon vanilla)

In a large cold mixing bowl, whip heavy cream and cheese with hand mixer or stand mixer with whisk attachment. Start on low speed and as the cream begins to thicken, increase speed. Add vanilla, then, gradually add sugar until soft peaks form.

makes one cheesecake

Other Topping Suggestions

Blackberries and Fresh Mint Leaves Lightly Macerated with Raspberry Liqueur (such as Chambord). Rinse and dry 1 pint blackberries and ¼ cup fresh mint leaves. In a small bowl gently stir berries, mint and 1 tablespoon raspberry liqueur. Allow to macerate at room temperature one hour before serving. Spoon berries over each slice and dollop with whipped mascarpone cream.

Strawberries Lightly Macerated with Grand Marnier. Follow the same instructions as with the blackberries above with strawberries and orange liqueur. Finish with a dollop of mascarpone cream. I like to garnish with a wedge of fresh orange, skin and pith removed, which compliments the orange liqueur. If you don't care for orange liqueur, good aged balsamic vinegar is also excellent for macerating strawberries.

CHOCOLATE SWIRL CHEESECAKE

For those chocolate *AND* cheesecake enthusiasts, this one's for you. Rich creamy cheesecake swirled with decadent dark chocolate. A chocolate lovers dream!

1½ cups graham cracker crumbs
½ cup light brown sugar *(organic)*

½ cup toasted almonds, slivered
½ cup unsalted butter, softened

Preheat oven to 350 degrees. Place almonds on a sheet pan and toast in the oven until golden brown, 5-8 minutes, turning once. Let them cool and grind in a food processor or spice grinder until fine. Combine with graham cracker crumbs, brown sugar and butter, pulsing in food processor, until just combined. Press into a spring form pan on the bottom and up all sides. Bake crust until lightly browned and set, 8-10 minutes. Cool completely on rack.

the filling

5 organic eggs
2 organic egg yolks
5 eight-ounce packages organic light cream cheese, room temperature
1½ cups organic cane sugar
1 teaspoon Madagascar vanilla extract

1 teaspoon freshly squeezed lemon juice
1 tablespoon freshly grated lemon zest
1 teaspoon freshly grated orange zest
6 ounces good bittersweet chocolate *(such as Ghiradelli)*

Raise oven temperature to 450 degrees. Prepare batter as directed in my **Basic Citrus Cheesecake** recipe. Pour 1/3 of the prepared batter into a separate bowl, set aside. Melt chocolate in a bowl placed over a medium saucepan of simmering water, or in the microwave. Allow the chocolate to cool to room temperature and whisk into the separate batter until smooth. Pour half of the original batter mixture into prepared spring form pan. Follow with chocolate batter, then re-maining original batter. With a smooth bladed knife, very carefully swirl the batter in a figure 8 until a marble pattern is formed. Be careful not to over swirl. Bake 15 minutes then reduce heat to 250 degrees and bake for 1 hour. Turn oven off, open the oven door and let cake continue to cook approximately 20 minutes until the center has set.

Cool on rack, then refrigerate at least 8 hours or overnight. Remove cake from spring form pan on a serving plate. Allow cake to come to room temperature before serving. When slicing, dip your knife into a tall glass of warm water and wipe with a towel in between each slice. Dollop with whipped cream and top with grated chocolate using a *Microplane* grater or shave thin strips of chocolate with a vegetable peeler over top.

whipped cream

Place 1 cup heavy whipping cream in a large cold bowl. Beat starting on medium speed, increasing speed as the cream begins to thicken. Slowly add ¼ cup sugar. Beat until whipped cream forms soft peaks.

makes one cheesecake

dessert

RICH CHOCOLATE SOUFFLÉ

serves 4

There is something about a warm chocolate dessert that is so soothing after a wonderful meal. Simple to prepare yet your guests will be swooning over this little bite of warm chocolate awesomeness. For a more elegant presentation, I like to serve with a Chocolate Crème Anglaise and/or fresh raspberries or blackberries; however, it is quite simply chocolate perfection just as it is.

6 ounces good bittersweet chocolate
(I recommend Ghirardelli, Valrhona, or Scharffen Berger)
4 large organic eggs, separated

1/4 cup organic cane sugar
1/8 teaspoon fresh lemon juice
1 tablespoon organic powdered sugar
4 sprigs of fresh mint *(optional)*

Preheat oven to 400 degrees. Melt chocolate in a bowl over a saucepan of simmering water or in the microwave, stirring often until just melted. Allow the chocolate to cool to room temperature. Spray 4 ramekins with butter flavor non-stick spray and sprinkle with a pinch of sugar. Beat egg whites with an electric mixer, or a stand mixer using the whisk attachment, until they begin to foam, then, add lemon juice. Add sugar a little at a time and continue to beat until stiff peaks form. Whisk egg yolks into the cooled chocolate and then 1/3 of the whites. Add remaining whites and fold into the chocolate mixture very gently. Scoop into ramekins with a large ice cream scoop.

Tap each ramekin on the counter and place on a sheet pan. Bake approximately 10 minutes. The soufflés will be browned and puffy on top and still slightly gooey on the inside. Remove ramekins from sheet pan and place on individual serving plates. Using a fine mesh strainer with 1 tablespoon powdered sugar, tap to sprinkle a little sugar the top of each soufflé before serving. Garnish each with a sprig of fresh mint if desired and serve immediately.

chocolate creme anglaise

1 cup milk
1/4 cup organic cane sugar

2 egg yolks
1 teaspoon good vanilla
(Madagascar bourbon vanilla)

Whisk together milk, sugar and egg yolks in a medium saucepan over medium heat, stirring constantly until it begins to thicken and sticks to the back of a wooden spoon. Pour into a medium bowl and stir in chocolate for a minute or two until melted. Add vanilla and whisk until well blended. Place in a large bowl with ice water and continue to whisk until cool. Cover and refrigerate 2-3 hours. Bring to room temperature before serving.

The Perfect Mint Julep

1 ounce simple syrup *(mint infused)*
   (1 cup water, 1 cup sugar, 1 bunch fresh mint)
2 ounces good Kentucky bourbon *(Makers Mark)*
Crushed ice, fresh sprig of mint

In a medium non-reactive saucepan over medium heat, stir 1 cup water and 1 cup sugar until all of the sugar has dissolved, simmer 3-5 minutes, stir. Remove from heat and add 1 bunch fresh mint, infusing 15-20 minutes. Strain into a small bowl, cover and refrigerate 2-4 hours. Fill a highball or silver julep cup with crushed ice.

Pour simple syrup over ice, then bourbon, gently stir. Add more ice if desired and a fresh sprig of mint.

KENTUCKY DERBY PIE

serves 6 to 8

Jeff is from Kentucky and has missed few Kentucky Derbies at Churchill Downs in his lifetime. Derby Pie is my favorite Kentucky institution, rich and chocolaty with crunchy pecans…sinfully delectable, especially with a mint julep! This is my version of the prized Kentucky tradition.

2 large organic eggs

1 cup organic cane sugar

½ cup *(1 stick)* unsalted butter

2 cups pecans *(1½ cups for pie; ½ cup for garnish)*

1 cup bittersweet chocolate chips *(Ghiardelli)*

1 cup all purpose organic flour

1 teaspoon good vanilla extract *(Madagascar bourbon vanilla)*

1 tablespoon good Kentucky bourbon

1 prepared piecrust *(recipe to follow)*

Preheat oven to 350 degrees. Bake crust with pie weights until just browned, 10-15 minutes. Cool on wire rack. Meanwhile, melt chocolate in an oven proof bowl in the oven (or in the microwave) and set aside to cool. Cream eggs, sugar and butter with electric mixer in a large bowl. Blend in chocolate, bourbon and vanilla, then add flour and blend until just combined. Fold nuts into batter and spread into prepared piecrust. Bake 40-45 minutes until set. Cool completely on a wire rack. Serve individual slices warm or at room temperature with a dollop of whipped cream and fresh mint leaves.

pie crust

2½ cups all purpose organic flour, chilled

1 cup *(2 sticks)* cold unsalted butter, cubed

1 teaspoon salt

1 teaspoon organic cane sugar

¼ to ½ cup ice water

Place dry ingredients into bowl of food processor. Add cubes of butter and process until the dough looks like coarse meal. Add ice water 1 teaspoon at a time through the feed tube with the processor running, until dough just holds together. Be careful not to over process. Pour dough out onto floured surface and work until just smooth. Divide into two equal disks. Wrap each in plastic wrap and chill at least one hour. The extra half can be stored in the freezer for another use later. Roll dough out on floured surface and line a 9-inch pie plate crimping the edges.

FRESH FRUIT CRUMBLE

serves 6 to 8

A warm, aromatic fresh fruit crumble is just plain comfort indulgence. I serve them for dessert year round using the fresh fruits that are in season. In summer I love the combination of peaches and blueberries, in the fall, apples and pears. Serve in a martini glass with a dollop of whipped mascarpone cream or a small scoop of vanilla ice cream drizzled with honey and toasted sliced almonds. Here are a few great crumble combos for any season! *(see next page)*

1 cup organic flour *(all purpose or whole grain)*
½ cup organic cane sugar
½ cup organic light brown sugar
½ cup oats
½ teaspoon kosher salt
½ tablespoon Vietnamese cinnamon
1 teaspoon ground cloves
1 teaspoon ground nutmeg
1 teaspoon ground ginger

½ cup sliced almonds *(or chopped walnuts)*
½ cup *(1 stick)* unsalted butter, cubed
5-6 cups fresh fruit *(combinations to follow)*
½ teaspoon kosher salt
1 teaspoon Vietnamese cinnamon
1 tablespoon fresh lemon zest
½ cup Amaretto *(almond liqueur)* or fresh lemon juice

Preheat oven to 400 degrees. In a large bowl, combine first 10 ingredients and the butter. Mix together with fingers or paddle attachment of a stand mixer until it resembles course meal. Set aside. Place fruit in a medium to large baking dish. Pour liqueur or lemon juice over fruit and evenly distribute lemon zest and salt. Sprinkle with a pinch of cinnamon and toss to coat evenly. Pour crumble over fruit. Top with more nuts if desired and drizzle with organic honey. Place a few thin pats of butter around the top of the crumble and bake for 45 minutes or until browned on top and the fruit is bubbling around the edges.

mascarpone cream

1 cup chilled heavy cream *(organic)*
½ cup Mascarpone cheese *(or cream cheese)*

¼ cup organic cane sugar
1 teaspoon good vanilla extract *(Madagascar bourbon vanilla)*

In a large cold mixing bowl, whip heavy cream and cheese with hand mixer or stand mixer with whisk attachment. Start on low speed and as the cream begins to thicken, increase speed. Add vanilla, then, gradually add sugar until soft peaks form.

variations on next page $\longrightarrow$

serves 6 to 8

...MORE CRUMBLES...

Follow crumble preparation steps on previous page.

Using the same basic crumble, here are a few more fruit crumble combinations sure to delight for every occasion. Be creative, have fun and come up with your own favorite combos!

Peach-Blueberry Crumble

My favorite crumble combo—especially when fresh peaches are in season and abundant. Warm with whipped mascarpone cream on top—simply amazing.

4 cups fresh peaches, *peeled and sliced*
1 cup fresh blueberries

Apple-Fig Crumble

I love the combination of apples and figs in late summer and early fall when figs are in season, though dried figs work just as well in this crumble. Topped off with whipped mascarpone cream or vanilla ice cream and a little sprinkle of cinnamon!

4-5 cups Granny Smith apples, *peeled, cored and sliced*
1 cup black mission or brown turkey figs, sliced, stems removed *(or 1 cup dried figs, thinly sliced, stems removed)*

**For a simple Apple Crumble use 5-6 cups Granny Smith apples, peeled, cored and sliced. Top with good vanilla ice cream—simple and delicious.

Mixed Berry Crumble

This is a great crumble in the summer when fresh berries are at their peak. Perfect for the Fourth of July served warm with plenty of homemade vanilla ice cream!

4-6 cups mixed berries *(any combination) (strawberries, hulled and sliced, blackberries, raspberries and/or blueberries)*

Pear-Cranberry Crumble *with crystalized ginger*

My traditional holiday crumble, it is delicious with pears, but apples are equally as delectable. The addition of whole fresh cranberries makes it festive and the warmth of the ginger brings this comfort dessert to another level. Topped with Dulce de Leche ice cream—pure holiday decadence!

4-5 cups fresh Bosc pears *(or Granny Smith apples) peeled, cored and sliced*
1 cup fresh cranberries, *whole*
2 tablespoons crystalized ginger, *coarsely chopped*

JOHNNY SHORTCAKE

Bahamian Johnnycake makes wonderful shortcake for your favorite summer fruits. I love the combination of peaches and/or blueberries, or just simple strawberry shortcake, always a family favorite.

4-6 cups fresh fruit in season
1¼ cup all purpose organic flour
¾ cup fine cornmeal
¼ cup organic cane sugar
1½ teaspoons baking powder
1 teaspoon fine sea salt crystals

2 large organic eggs
¾ cup 2% milk
¼ cup light molasses
3 tablespoons extra light olive oil
Raw organic sugar *(to sprinkle on top)*

Slice fruit into 1/8 inch slices, sprinkle with sugar and stir. Cover and refrigerate, allowing the fruit and sugar to macerate, for one hour or until ready to serve. Preheat oven to 325 degrees. Spray two loaf pans with non-stick spray. Whisk dry ingredients together, then add eggs, milk, molasses and olive oil. Divide batter into the two pans and sprinkle with raw sugar. Bake 40-45 minutes until golden brown and toothpick in center comes out clean. Cool in pans on wire rack 10 minutes, then turn out of pan. Slice in approximately 1-inch slices while still warm and place 1 slice on each individual serving plate. Spoon fruit over Johnnycake and add a second slice over top. Add more fruit and top with fresh whipped cream.

whipped cream

Place 1 cup heavy whipping cream in a large cold bowl. Beat starting on medium speed, increasing speed as the cream begins to thicken. Slowly add ¼ cup sugar. Beat until whipped cream forms soft peaks.

serves 4 to 6

GEORGIA PECAN TART

Our dear friends the Tidwell's have a beautiful pecan farm in South Georgia. I have never tasted a better pecan. They harvest in late November, just in time for the holidays. These pecans are sweet, rich and nutty, perfect for this super rich and scrumptious tart.

Prepared tart crust (a good store bought crust works fine too, such as Pillsbury)

3 large organic eggs

2/3 cup organic cane sugar

1 cup light corn syrup (Karo)

¼ cup unsalted butter, melted

3 tablespoons orange liqueur (Grand Marnier)

1 teaspoon Madagascar vanilla extract

1 tablespoon fresh orange zest

Pinch kosher salt

1-2 cups pecan halves

Preheat oven to 375 degrees. Roll out pastry and line a 9-inch tart pan, eliminating excess crust by taking your rolling pin over the top edge of pan. Bake crust with pastry beads, 10-15 minutes, until just browned. Whisk together sugar, corn syrup and butter in a medium bowl. Whisk the eggs in one at a time, then add liqueur, vanilla, orange zest and salt, mix well. At this point you can simply fold the pecans into the batter and pour into the prepared tart shell or pour the batter into prepared crust and arrange pecans on top in a decorative pattern. I like a circular pattern starting with the outside edge, working toward the center. Bake 40-50 minutes until the tart is set in the center. Cool on a wire rack and serve with whipped cream or serve warm with good vanilla ice cream.

whipped cream

Place 1 cup heavy whipping cream in a large cold bowl. Beat starting on medium speed, increasing speed as the cream begins to thicken. Slowly add ¼ cup sugar. Beat until whipped cream forms soft peaks.

tart crust

¼ cup (½ stick) unsalted butter, cut into ½ inch cubes and chilled

1¼ cup all purpose flour, chilled

½ teaspoon kosher salt, chilled

¼ cup mascarpone cheese, chilled (or cream cheese)

½ teaspoon sugar, chilled

1/8 - ¼ cup ice water

Place all ingredients in food processor, except water and pulse to a course meal consistency. Gradually add water, 1 tablespoon at a time until dough forms a into ball. Chill in a flat round in plastic wrap at least 30 minutes.

serves 6 to 8

RED VELVET CUPCAKES

When I was growing up we celebrated the 4th of July with John Philip Sousa marches and Red Velvet Cake. I still use my mother's rich and delicious cake recipe, but the frosting is all Gigi...mascarpone and cream cheese, unsalted butter and Madagascar bourbon vanilla. Sousa would have marched all the way to my house for one of these!

2 cups all purpose organic flour *(or 2½ cups cake flour)*

2 tablespoons good unsweetened cocoa *(Pernigotti)*

1 teaspoon salt

1½ cups organic cane sugar

1½ cups extra light olive oil

2 large eggs

1-2 tablespoons red food coloring

1 teaspoon pure vanilla extract *(Madagascar Bourbon)*

1 cup buttermilk

1½ teaspoons baking soda

2 teaspoons white vinegar

Preheat oven to 350 degrees. Prepare muffin pan by spraying cups with non-stick spray or lining with paper muffin cups. Sift together flour, cocoa and salt. With the paddle attachment of stand mixer (or electric mixer) blend sugar and oil until combined. Add eggs one at a time, then food coloring and vanilla. On low speed, (stir) add flour mixture 1/3 at a time alternating with buttermilk. Stir baking soda and vinegar together in a small bowl and add to batter. Mix only until combined. Fill muffin cups ¾ full with ice cream scoop and bake 15-20 minutes until toothpick comes out clean. Cool in pan on wire rack 5-10 minutes. Carefully remove cupcakes from muffin pan and cool completely on wire rack. Top with frosting. I like to use a round tip and pastry bag starting around the outside edge and working to the center.

the frosting

4 ounces each cream cheese and mascarpone cheese *(or 8 oz. cream cheese)*

1½ teaspoons Madagascar bourbon vanilla

½ cup unsalted butter, softened

2½ cups organic confectioners *(powdered)* **sugar**

In a medium bowl, cream vanilla and cheeses with a hand mixer. Add butter and mix until creamy. Add sugar ¼ cup at a time and continue to mix until fluffy.

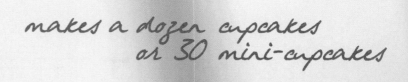

makes a dozen cupcakes
or 30 mini-cupcakes

TIRAMISU TRIFLE

Tiramisu is a semi-freddo dessert, *(cold but not frozen)*, originating in the Veneto region of northern Italy. Traditionally made with a raw egg yolk custard and lady finger biscuits soaked in espresso. Mine is a little different. I keep the lady fingers, but use mascarpone cream instead of the heavy custard, and a touch of Amaretto for a nice hint of almond flavor. Light, airy, and *so decedente'!*

Mascarpone Cream
(recipe below)

3 tablespoons Amaretto
  (almond liqueur)

¾ cup espresso or strong coffee

24 Lady Fingers

6 ounces grated bittersweet chocolate
  (Ghiradelli)

1 tablespoon good cocoa powder
  (Perignotti)

Combine coffee and liqueur in a glass measuring bowl with a pour spout (Pyrex). Line the bottom of a trifle dish with Lady Fingers and drizzle with coffee mixture. Spoon ¼ of the mascarpone cream overtop and spread evenly to cover the lady fingers. Top with a sprinkling of grated chocolate. Repeat starting with Lady Fingers to form 4 layers finishing with mascarpone cream. Place cocoa in a fine mesh strainer and sprinkle over top of the trifle. Cover and chill at least 2 hours.

mascarpone cream

12 ounces mascarpone cheese

3 cups heavy cream

¾ cup sugar

1 tablespoon almond liqueur
  (Amaretto)

special occasions

special

OCCASION MENUS

RUSTIC THANKSGIVING FEAST

We start Thanksgiving Day with a light breakfast with a fresh seasonal fruit salad drizzled with honey and my Pumpkin-Cranberry Muffins fresh from the oven. The warm aroma of holiday spice is the perfect way to start the day. Then the fun begins in the kitchen preparing a casual yet elegant Thanksgiving Dinner. Simple dishes that flavorfully compliment one another, and, most can be prepared in advance to avoid the last minute scurry of getting a Thanksgiving feast prepared and on the table all at one time.

Festive Goat Cheese Salad *(pg. 50)*
Roasted Turkey with White Wine Gravy *(see below & 138)*
Cranberry Sauce *(pg. 200)*
Ciabatta~Cornbread Stuffing *(pg. 198)*

Mashed Yukon Potatoes *(pg. 160)*
Roasted Brussel Sprouts *(pg. 166)*
Pear-Cranberry Crumble *(pg. 185)*
Georgia Pecan Tart *(pg. 188)*

Select a turkey using the 1½ to 2 pounds/person rule. Follow my *Easy Roasted Chicken* recipe to roast a perfect Thanksgiving turkey *(pg. 138)*. You will want to roast the turkey 13 minutes per pound until internal temperature is 165 throughout. Baste the turkey with the pan juices every 45 minutes or so by removing from the oven, closing the oven door to maintain heat. Protect the breast with foil if necessary to keep from getting too brown. For added flavor, baste the turkey approximately 15 minutes before it is to be done by brushing generously with basting sauce. Cover loosely with foil. Allow the turkey to rest at least 30 minutes before carving. Prepare white wine gravy *(Easy Roasted Chicken recipe, Pg 138)*.

the basting sauce

1 tablespoon extra virgin olive oil
1 Granny Smith apple peeled, cored and sliced
1 small onion, rough chop

1 bunch fresh sage leaves
4 cloves garlic, peeled and chopped
½ cup organic cane sugar
1 cup white wine vinegar

In a medium saucepan, heat olive oil over medium high heat. Add onion and cook until soft. Add remaining ingredients and simmer over medium heat until tender. Remove from heat and allow to cool to room temperature. Pour into food processor or blender and puree until smooth.

The Brussel Sprouts
Rinse and halve brussel sprouts, removing stems and outer leaves. Follow my *Roasted Winter Vegetable* recipe on page (166). Top with crumbled crispy bacon if desired before serving.

serves 6 to 8

CIABATTA~CORNBREAD STUFFING *serves 8 to 10*

Jeff's favorite part of Thanksgiving dinner is this stuffing. We once served it for Thanksgiving dinner with the Swiss Ambassador to the United States, who described it as "gorgeous flavor." I think I would have to agree.

4 cups Ciabatta bread, cubed and toasted

4 cups cornbread cubed and toasted

¼ cup unsalted butter

1 tablespoon extra virgin olive oil

1 large onion

1 medium shallot

4 celery ribs

4 cloves garlic

1 cup flat leaf parsley, divided

2 tablespoons fresh sage leaves

1 tablespoon fresh thyme leaves

1 cup Parmigiano Reggiano cheese, plus more for topping

4 oz. prosciutto, chopped

3 eggs

2-3 cups organic low sodium chicken or vegetable broth

Prepare a large baking dish with non-stick cooking spray and set aside. Preheat oven to 400 degrees. Cut ciabatta and cornbread into 1-inch cubes. Arrange on a sheet pan and season lightly with salt and pepper. Drizzle with olive oil and toast in the oven until slightly brown and dry, 10-15 minutes.

Melt butter in large sauté pan with 1 tablespoon extra virgin olive oil over medium heat. Add onion, shallots, celery and cook until vegetables are soft. Add garlic and cook one minute more. Next, add sage, thyme, ½ cup flat leaf parsley and prosciutto. Cook another minute, stirring to combine all ingredients. Add to toasted bread cubes.

Whisk eggs with cheese, remaining ½ cup parsley and 1 cup of broth. Pour over bread mixture and toss to combine. Add 2 cups of broth and toss well to combine all ingredients. Pour evenly into prepared baking dish. Season to taste with course salt and freshly ground pepper. Top with freshly grated Parmigiano Reggiano cheese and a drizzle of extra virgin olive oil. Bake until puffy and browned on top, 40-50, minutes.

HOLIDAY CRANBERRY SAUCE

No holiday dinner table is complete without fresh cranberry sauce. This one is sweet and tart, with just enough warm aromatic spice and a hint of orange. A perfect compliment to any holiday meal and fantastic on a leftover turkey sandwich!

12 oz. fresh cranberries

½ cup Grand Marnier (orange liqueur)

¼ cup organic cane sugar

3 strips orange or tangerine zest

1 cinnamon stick

¼ teaspoon ground cloves

Bring all ingredients to a medium simmer in a heavy, non-reactive saucepan, stirring occasionally until most all of the cranberries have burst, approximately 12-15 minutes. Remove from heat and allow to cool in saucepan.

Remove cinnamon stick and transfer to a serving bowl. Cranberry Sauce can be made 3 days ahead and refrigerated until serving time.

FESTIVE HOLIDAY MENU

holiday breakfast

Start the day with a traditional holiday chestnut panettone …*Gigi style!*

- **Panettone French Toast** *(pg. 204)*
- **Cantaloupe Wedges Wrapped in Prosciutto**
- **Mimosa or Gigi Bellini** *(pg. 17)*

festive holiday dinner *serves 6 to 8*

This l'orange inspired menu is perfect for a festive Christmas holiday celebration.

- **Sweet Corn Chowder with Lobster** *(pg. 206)*
- **Fennel~Orange Salad** *(pg. 32)*
- **Porc l'orange** *(pg. 208)*
- **Mashed Potatoes** *(pg. 160)*
- **Haricots Verts Amandine** *(pg. 158)*
- **Coconut Crème Cupcakes** *(pg. 210)*

serves 6 to 8

PANETTONE FRENCH TOAST

My favorite Christmas Breakfast is a Chestnut Panettone French Toast. My version has a sweet kick…Grand Marnier (orange liqueur). Served with a festive mimosa, nothing starts the holiday more merrily!

1 loaf Chestnut Panettone
6 eggs *(organic optional)*
2 cups milk, 2%
1 teaspoon Vietnamese cinnamon
½ teaspoon freshly grated nutmeg
2 tablespoons Grand Marnier
Grated zest of 1 orange

Preheat oven to 200 degrees. Place serving plates in the oven and turn oven off. Cut Panettone into one inch slices. Save the end pieces for toast later! In a large mixing bowl, whisk eggs, milk, cinnamon, nutmeg, orange liqueur and zest. Pour into a large flat dish (i.e. 9 x 13 baking dish). Lightly grease griddle or pan with unsalted butter and bring to medium high heat. Pam spray (or other non-stick cooking spray) is also fine to grease the cooking surface.

When the griddle is hot, soak both sides of Panettone slices in egg mixture, wiping off excess, and cook until brown, 2 minutes per side. Place on heated plate and cover with foil to keep warm while cooking the remaining slices.

to serve

½ cup organic powdered sugar
2 cups 100% Pure Maple Syrup *(organic)*
1 Tablespoon orange liqueur *(Grand Marnier)*

Stir one tablespoon orange liqueur into maple syrup. Heat through in a small saucepan over medium low heat (or in the microwave). Place 1-2 slices of french toast on each serving plate. Dust with powdered sugar, using a fine mesh strainer.

Serve with warm syrup and cold mimosas!

SWEET CORN CHOWDER WITH LOBSTER

A warm and special way to begin a festive holiday celebration dinner, or a wonderful chowder for a stand alone meal. Rich and creamy, a satisfying and decadent starter or entrée.

2 eight oz. lobster tails, broiled
(See my recipe, pg. 106)

8 cups frozen yellow corn, organic
(thawed)

3 cups organic low sodium vegetable broth

2 cups organic low sodium chicken broth

2 cups scallions (green onions), finely chopped, white parts only

3 tablespoons extra virgin olive oil

½ cup heavy cream

¼-½ teaspoon cayenne pepper
(to taste)

2 tablespoons flat leaf parsley, chopped

2 tablespoons freshly chopped chives

Chopped crispy bacon, for finishing
(optional)

Broil lobster tails according to my recipe and cut into bite size pieces when cooled. Set aside. In a blender or food processor, puree 6 cups corn with 2 cups chicken broth until smooth with a few remaining kernels of corn left in tact. In a large stock pot over medium heat add olive oil and onions and sauté until soft, 3-5 minutes. Add vegetable broth and cayenne pepper and simmer 5-10 minutes. Stir in corn puree and cream and season to taste with kosher salt and freshly ground black pepper. Add remaining corn kernels and continue to simmer stirring occasionally, 10-15 minutes.

To serve, ladle chowder into individual soup bowls. Add reserved lobster meat and finish with a sprinkling of chives and parsley. Add crumbled crispy bacon if desired.

serves 4 to 6

serves 4 to 6

PORC L'ORANGE

This beautiful pork tenderloin is as delicious as it is pleasing to the eye.
Sweet and savory and so tender, it simply melts in your mouth.

2½ pound pork tenderloin roast
2 tablespoons extra virgin olive oil
Kosher salt and freshly ground pepper to taste

Preheat oven to 425 degrees. Prepare basting sauce and set aside. Heat olive oil in roasting pan on medium high heat. Pat pork tenderloin dry with paper towels and season with kosher salt and pepper. Sear in olive oil on all sides until nicely browned. Brush generously with basting sauce and roast until internal temperature reaches 145 degrees, medium, about 30 minutes, basting occasionally while it is roasting. Remove pork to a cutting board and cover loosely with foil to rest. Reserve pan drippings and prepare finishing sauce. While the sauce is reducing, slice pork into 1-2 inch slices, slightly on the diagonal. Place on a serving platter and garnish with fresh rosemary stalks. Spoon finishing sauce over the slices.

basting sauce

1 tablespoon unsalted butter
½ cup good orange marmalade
2 tablespoons country Dijon mustard
1 tablespoon fresh rosemary leaves, finely chopped

2 cloves garlic, minced
1 tablespoon fresh thyme leaves
1 teaspoon Herbs de Provence
1 teaspoon orange liqueur *(Grand Marnier)*

Melt butter in a medium saucepan over medium low heat. Add remaining ingredients and stir together. Simmer for 5 minutes. Brush on pork tenderloin every 10 minutes while it is roasting.

the finishing sauce

Reserved pan drippings
½ cup dry white wine *(or champagne)*
1 teaspoon orange liqueur *(Grand Marnier)*

1 tablespoon unsalted butter
1 tablespoon flat leaf parsley, chopped

Bring pan drippings to a simmer over medium heat. Add wine and orange liqueur and reduce by half, stirring to loosen the browned bits of flavor on the bottom of the pan. Add butter and swirl until melted. Finish with parsley and spoon over tenderloin slices.

makes one dozen

COCONUT CRÈME CUPCAKES

My Jeff's favorite special occasion dessert is Coconut Crème Cake. So, for his birthday and Christmas dinner, it is always Coconut Crème Cupcakes. Cupcakes make serving dessert so easy. Festively decorate a serving platter, or cake stand and simply pass them around the table after dinner. They also freeze just beautifully keeping them fresh for a sweet treat later.

1½ cups organic all purpose flour
1 teaspoon baking powder
½ teaspoon salt
1½ cup unsalted butter
1¼ cup organic cane sugar

1 teaspoon Madagascar vanilla extract
½ cup coconut milk
2 eggs plus 1 egg yolk
¾ cup shredded coconut *(sweetened)*

Preheat oven to 350 degrees. Spray muffin cups with non-stick baking spray, or line with cupcake liners. Mix dry ingredients well and set aside. Beat butter and sugar with paddle attachment of stand mixer until light and fluffy. Beat in vanilla and scrape down sides of bowl. Add dry ingredients slowly, beating at low speed, alternating with coconut milk until just combined. Using an ice cream scoop, fill muffins cups ¾ full (approximately ¼ cup of batter). Bake until nicely golden brown and toothpick inserted in center comes out clean, 18-22 minutes. Cool pan on wire rack 2-3 minutes, then using a smooth bladed knife to loosen edges remove cupcakes from pan and move to rack to cool completely. Frost with coconut crème frosting and sprinkle with toasted coconut. Shown frosted with a large closed star tip and pastry bag.

coconut crème frosting

4 ounces cream cheese
4 ounces mascarpone cheese
¾ cups unsalted butter, softened
1 teaspoon vanilla extract

2¾ cups organic powdered sugar
1 cup shredded coconut, sweetened
1 cup toasted coconut for finishing

Using paddle attachment of stand mixer, blend the cheeses, butter and vanilla until creamy. Add the powdered sugar ¼ cup at a time and blend until smooth. Add coconut and mix on low (stir) until well combined.

NEW YEAR'S EVE SOIREE

Champagne and caviar to ring in the New Year…what could be finer? Well, maybe a little lobster tail and pasta to follow.

Classic Caviar on Buckwheat Blinis with Crème Fraiche
Lobster Beurre Blanc *(pg. 214)*
Meyer Lemon Vermicelli *(pg. 215)*
Tiramisu Trifle *(pg. 192)*

the blinis

Heat a non-stick sauté pan or griddle over medium high heat. In a medium bowl, add ¾ cup buckwheat pancake mix, ½ cup milk, 1 egg and whisk until just combined. Whisk in 1 tablespoon extra light olive oil. Spoon 1 tablespoon batter onto the hot surface and cook until bubbles form on the edges. Turn and cook until cooked through, about a minute. Remove to a plate and continue until all of the blinis are cooked. Can be made ahead and refrigerated (or frozen in Ziploc baggies) until ready to serve. Bring blinis to room temperature and spoon with a dollop of crème fraiche. Top with a spoonful of caviar and serve with a lovely glass of champagne.

NEW YEAR'S DAY
celebration brunch

The Tournament of Roses Parade, Bloody Mary's and Mimosas with eggs benedict and lobster, now that's a great New Year's Day celebration! I always prepare an extra lobster tail or two on New Year's Eve so that I am sure to have plenty left for brunch on New Year's Day. A deliciously decadent start to the New Year!

Lobster Benedict *(pg. 216)*
Roasted Asparagus *(pg. 150)*
Champagne or Mimosas

LOBSTER BEURRE BLANC

serves 2

We always celebrate New Year's Eve at home with champagne, caviar and this wonderfully rich lobster beurre blanc served with a light vermicelli pasta and side of roasted asparagus *(accompaniments & tasteful sides)*. The ultimate celebratory feast!

2 lobster tails, 8 ounces each, broiled or grilled

1 medium shallot, finely chopped

2 cups dry champagne

2 tablespoons white wine vinegar

1 tablespoon Meyer lemon juice

½ teaspoon black peppercorns

1 cup unsalted butter, cut into 1 tablespoon pieces

1 tablespoon flat leaf parsley, finely chopped

1 tablespoon freshly chopped chives

1 tablespoon Meyer lemon zest

½-1 teaspoon kosher salt *(to taste)*

Broil or grill lobster tails (see recipe, pg. 106). Meanwhile, heat a medium saucepan over medium high heat and add shallot, champagne, vinegar and peppercorns. Briskly simmer (just below boiling point) until the liquid is reduced to ¼ cup, 15-20 minutes, remove from heat and allow to cool slightly. Reduce heat to medium low and rewarm the liquid. Whisk in butter, one tablespoon at a time. After all of the butter is combined, remove from heat and whisk in Meyer lemon juice. Season to taste with kosher salt. Place lobster tails on individual serving plates and spoon beurre blanc around and over top lobster tails. Sprinkle with parsley, chives and Meyer lemon zest. Pour extra sauce in a sauce boat and serve with the lobster.

the vermicelli

½ **pound vermicelli** *(very thin spaghetti)*

½ **cup unsalted butter, room temperature**

¼ **cup Meyer lemon juice**

1 tablespoon Meyer lemon zest

1 teaspoon fresh chopped chives

Course sea salt

Freshly ground pepper

Place butter, lemon juice and zest in a large bowl. Cook pasta according to package directions. Take pasta directly from pasta water to bowl using tongs or a pasta spoon. Toss well with butter and lemon and season with salt and pepper to taste. Serve immediately alongside lobster tails with a sprinkling of chives.

LOBSTER BENEDICT

serves 2

Nothing says special occasion like lobster and this special dish is up for the occasion. It is our holiday tradition for a breakfast or brunch and with a chilled mimosa or glass of champagne—*an extraordinary start to any festive celebration.*

4 large eggs, poached
  (organic free range)

2 English muffins, halved, toasted and buttered

1-2 grilled or broiled lobster tails
  (see recipe, pg. 106)

1 tablespoon flat leaf parsley, finely chopped

1 tablespoon fresh lemon zest

Lobster cream sauce, *(recipe below)*

Kosher salt and freshly ground pepper to taste

Cook lobster according to recipe. When cool enough to touch, cut into bite size pieces, about one inch cubes and set aside. Meanwhile, prepare sauce and poach the eggs. I like to use silicon egg poaching cups for poaching eggs. It makes poaching eggs so simple and the eggs turn out perfect every time. Simply spray the egg poaching cups with non-stick cooking spray and carefully fill each with one egg. Fill a medium saucepan or deep sauté pan with 1½ inches of water and a pinch of kosher salt. Bring water to a simmer over medium to medium-high heat and gently place eggs in their cups into the water. Poach eggs until whites are firm and yolks are still runny, 5-7 minutes, or until desired consistency. To speed the process, tent loosely with foil and poach for 3-5 minutes.

While the eggs are poaching, add the lobster meat to the finished sauce, just to heat through. When the eggs are poached to your liking, they can be spooned directly from the poaching cups right onto English muffin halves.

assembly

Place 2 toasted and buttered English muffin halves on each of two serving plates. Carefully spoon a poached egg on top of each half, directly from its poaching cup. Season with salt and pepper and spoon lobster sauce generously over each egg. To finish, sprinkle with lemon zest, fresh chopped parsley and freshly ground pepper. Serve with a tall cool mimosa or "Gigi Bellini!"

lobster cream sauce

2 tablespoons unsalted butter

2 tablespoons all purpose flour

1 cup milk at room temperature
  (2% milk fat)

1 tablespoon lemon zest

1 tablespoon fresh lemon juice

1 egg yolk

½ teaspoon kosher salt and freshly ground pepper to taste

¼ teaspoon nutmeg, freshly grated

1 tablespoon flat leaf *(Italian)* **parsley**

Reserved cooked lobster meat

Melt butter in a small saucepan over medium heat. Sprinkle flour evenly into butter and whisk until smooth. Slowly add milk whisking constantly until well combined. Cook over medium heat continuing to stir. When the sauce begins to thicken, add lemon zest, nutmeg, salt and pepper. Continue to stir with whisk until sauce is thick and creamy. Remove from heat and quickly whisk the egg yolk into the sauce. Whisk in lemon juice and add reserved lobster meat, stirring to combine. When the lobster meat has heated through, spoon sauce over eggs and serve as directed.

VALENTINE'S DAY FOR TWO

Call me a hopeless romantic, but Valentine's Day is my absolute favorite day of the year, champagne, chocolate, roses and 100+ renditions of "My Funny Valentine" playing all day and into the night. From Frank Sinatra to Chaka Khan, Miles Davis, Rap and everything in between!

breakfast

We start the day with decadent Chocolate Waffles. Even the kids will want one of these! A fun family breakfast or romantic breakfast any day of the year.

Chocolate Waffles *(pg. 220)*
Chocolate Covered Strawberries
Champagne

the strawberries

Rinse 1 pound of fresh strawberries and dry thoroughly with paper towels, keeping stems in tact. Melt 6 ounces of good bittersweet chocolate or 6 ounces bittersweet chocolate chips *(Ghiradelli)* in a medium bowl over a saucepan of simmering water, stirring constantly with a rubber spatula until melted and smooth. Or, melt in the microwave, in a microwave safe bowl, in 30-second increments, stirring in between until completely melted and smooth. Using the stem as a handle, dip each strawberry into the warm chocolate and swirl until all sides are coated. Place on a sheet of wax or parchment paper until the chocolate has reset, 20-25 minutes. Serve immediately, or make ahead and refrigerate until ready to serve.

VALENTINE'S DAY
—dinner for two

May I recommend my *Chateaubriand for Two* and *Rich Chocolate Soufflé* to complete a perfect Valentines Day of culinary delights!

Chateaubriand *(pg. 222)*

Roasted Winter Vegetables *(pg. 166)*

Chocolate Souffle' *(pg. 178)*

Red roses and your favorite bottle of red wine!

CHOCOLATE WAFFLES

serves 2

Call me a hopeless romantic, but Valentine's Day is my favorite day of the year. We start the day with decadent Chocolate Waffles and champagne, listening to my 100 plus renditions of *"My Funny Valentine."* A beautiful romantic breakfast any day of the year.

1 cup original Bisquick baking mix
¾ cup good unsweetened cocoa
   (Pernigotti)
½ cup organic cane sugar
¾ cup milk

1 teaspoon vanilla extract
   (Madagascar bourbon vanilla)
1 tablespoon extra light olive oil
1 egg

Preheat oven to 250 degrees. Coat waffle iron with non-stick spray and heat until very hot. In a medium bowl, whisk dry ingredients together. Add wet ingredients and stir until just combined, do not overmix. Pour approximately ½ cup batter into the center for each waffle in hot waffle iron, close lid and cook 3-5 minutes until steaming stops. Carefully remove waffles and keep warm in the oven until all of the waffles have been cooked.

Dust with powdered sugar and serve with strawberries and whipped mascarpone cream; or butter and your favorite syrup.

mascarpone cream

1 cup chilled heavy cream *(organic)*
½ cup mascarpone cheese *(or cream cheese)*
¼ cup organic cane sugar
1 teaspoon good vanilla extract *(Madagascar bourbon vanilla)*

In a cold large mixing bowl, whip heavy cream and cheese with hand mixer or stand mixer with whisk attachment. Start on low speed and as the cream begins to thicken, increase speed. Add vanilla, then gradually add sugar and continue to beat until soft peaks form.

waffles

special occasion

CHATEAUBRIAND FOR TWO

I don't know of a more romantic dinner for two than a Chateaubriand. This slow roasted tenderloin is so tender and full of flavor, not to mention incredibly simple to prepare. Use a Certified Angus beef tenderloin and have the butcher trim and tie it at 1-inch intervals. A perfect special occasion dinner just for the two of you!

1½ pounds center cut portion of beef tenderloin, trimmed and tied
Extra virgin olive oil

4 sprigs of fresh thyme
Kosher salt and fresh ground pepper to taste

Preheat oven to 275 degrees. Brush tenderloin all over with olive oil. Season with salt and pepper and sear all sides in a roasting pan or large oven proof sauté pan over high heat. Slide thyme under the string and brush again with olive oil. Season generously with more salt and pepper and insert roasting thermometer. Roast until internal temperature is 130 to 135 degrees for medium rare, 1 to 1½ hours. Remove from oven and place tenderloin on a cutting board to rest, reserving pan drippings. Allow the meat to sit 15-20 minutes tented loosely with foil. Meanwhile, prepare sauce.

the sauce

1 cup sliced mushrooms *(cremini or shitake)*
1 tablespoon each, extra virgin olive oil and unsalted butter
1 tablespoon thyme leaves *(plus more for finishing)*

1 tablespoon chives, finely chopped
½ cup dry red wine
1 small shallot, thinly sliced into rings
1½ cups vegetable broth
Roux *(1 Tablespoon flour in ¼ cup water, whisked in a small bowl)*

In a small sauté pan cook mushrooms in olive oil and butter with shallot and thyme. Season with salt and pepper to taste. When mushrooms have begun to caramelize, remove from heat and set aside. Place roasting pan with pan drippings over medium heat. Add red wine and stir, loosening the browned bits that may be sticking to the bottom of the pan. Add shallot and vegetable broth and stir while the liquid reduces, 2-3 minutes. While still simmering, add the roux and whisk until thickened. Remove from heat and add mushrooms.

Slice tenderloin into 1-inch slices, and place 2 slices on each individual serving plate. Spoon the sauce around the tenderloin and garnish with chopped chives and fresh thyme leaves. If you are serving with my roasted vegetables, you can prepare the vegetables in advance, then while the meat is resting, with the oven off, place the vegetables back into the oven to heat through while you prepare your sauce.

CASUAL SPRING EASTER DINNER

When spring is in the air so are the colorful early harvest spring vegetables. Combined with a rack of lamb and of course a sweet chocolate finish, this traditional Easter menu is sure to delight. Don't forget to make extra deviled eggs!

Deviled Eggs
Colorado Rack of Lamb *(pg. 128)*
Penne with Spring Vegetables *(pg. 226)*
Chocolate Swirl Cheesecake *(pg. 176)*

serves 6 to 8

the eggs

One dozen fresh organic eggs
½ cup mayonnaise
2 teaspoons Dijon mustard
2 tablespoon yellow mustard
1 teaspoon sweet pickle juice

Kosher salt and fresh ground pepper to taste
Paprika for finishing
Fresh chives, finely chopped *(if desired)*

Place eggs a large saucepan with enough water to cover the eggs and a generous pinch of kosher salt. Bring to a boil over high heat and cook for 8 minutes. Remove from heat and cover, allowing the eggs to rest for 20-25 minutes. Rinse with cold water and carefully crack and peel eggs. Slice in half lengthwise with a smooth bladed knife and place the yolks in a medium bowl, whites on a serving plate. Smash the yolks with the beaters on an electric mixer and add mayo, mustards and pickle juice. Beat with electric mixer on medium speed until well combined and creamy. Season to taste with salt and pepper and thoroughly combine. Spoon creamy yolk mixture into a pastry bag or a Ziploc baggie, pressing the mixture into one corner. Snip the corner of the Ziploc baggie with a pair of kitchen shears and fill each egg white half with the yolk mixture, 1-2 teaspoons of filling in each one. Sprinkle with paprika and finely chopped chives if desired.

PENNE WITH SPRING VEGETABLES

Fresh spring vegetables are so colorful and springy! Served with penne pasta and tossed in an aromatic pesto sauce. This dish is a beautiful accompaniment to my *Colorado Rack of Lamb*.

serves 6 to 8

1 pound penne pasta
1 cup sugar snap peas
1 cup carrots
1 cup asparagus spears, chopped into 1-inch pieces
1 cup brussel sprouts, halved
1 cup broccoli, head only, chopped in 1-inch pieces

½ cup scallions (green onions) finely chopped
1 cup toasted pine nuts
½-1 cup Parmigiano-Reggiano cheese, freshly grated
Julienne of fresh basil
Kosher salt and freshly ground pepper to taste

Clean vegetables and cut into 1-inch pieces. Blanch in boiling salted water until tender, but still crisp, 2-3 minutes. Immerse immediately in an ice bath to stop the cooking and help the vegetables retain their beautiful color, set aside. Cook pasta according to package directions and move to a large bowl with a slotted spoon, reserving cooking liquid. While pasta is cooking, prepare pesto. Pour ¾ cup of the pesto over the pasta and toss well. Add ¼ to ½ cup pasta water and toss until the sauce is creamy and the pasta is thoroughly coasted with sauce.

Add vegetables and remaining pesto and toss until thoroughly combined. Pour into a serving dish and season to taste with salt and pepper. Finish with more grated Parmigiano-Reggiano cheese and julienne of fresh basil.

fresh herb pesto

1 large garlic clove
1 tablespoon walnuts
1 tablespoon pine nuts
½ cup basil leaves
½ cup cilantro leaves
¼ cup flat leaf parsley

1 teaspoon lemon juice
1 tablespoon lemon zest
¾ cup extra virgin olive oil
¼ cup Parmigiano-Reggiano cheese
½ teaspoon each, course sea salt and freshly ground pepper

In a food processor, combine nuts and garlic and pulse until finely chopped. Add basil, cilantro, parsley, salt and pepper and pulse until leaves are finely chopped. Stream olive oil through the feeding tube and process until smooth. Add cheese and pulse until combined.

SUMMER HOLIDAY BBQ

Whether a special summer holiday, or just another weekend of summer fun with friends and family, this menu offers a different twist to traditional burgers and dogs but no more difficult to prepare. Grilled shrimp cocktail, marinated flank steak, tangy potato salad, finished with a delicious fruit crumble and ice cream. Fire up the Barbie!

Rosemary Shrimp Cocktail *(pg. 78)*
Steak Victor with Herbed Butter *(pg. 230)*
Mediterranean Potato Salad *(pg. 162)*
Grilled Corn on the Cob *(below)*
Peach & Blueberry Crumble with vanilla ice cream *(pg. 185)*

grilling corn

Pull the husk back from each ear, far enough to remove the silk, but do not remove entirely. Remove silk from the corn and rinse thoroughly. Roll the husks back to the top of each ear and soak in a large bowl of cold water, 5-10 minutes. Heat grill to medium high and lay corn in its husk directly on the grates of the grill. Cook 15-20 minutes, turning every 5 minutes, until the corn is steamed through. Remove husks and serve with herbed butter. If you'd like the grill marks on the corn, simply place back on the grill after removing the husk and sear on all sides 1-2 minutes.

STEAK VICTOR

This is the ideal marinade for a flank steak or London broil (top round). For an appetizing change of pace, serve this flavorful dish for your next barbeque with my tangy Mediterranean potato salad and grilled corn on the cob with herbed butter.

2-3 pounds flank steak or London broil
¾ cup extra virgin olive oil
Zest of 1 lime
¼ cup fresh squeezed lime juice
¼ cup Cognac or Brandy
1 tablespoon Worcestershire Sauce
2 garlic cloves, minced

1 teaspoon dried oregano
1 tablespoon fresh rosemary, finely chopped
1 tablespoon fresh thyme, finely chopped
1 teaspoon Kosher salt
½ teaspoon ground pepper

Generously season both sides of meat with kosher salt and pepper. In a small bowl whisk together next 11 ingredients. Place meat in a large Ziploc bag or dish for marinating. Pour marinade over meat and allow it to sit in the refrigerator for at least 8 hours or overnight. Turn at least once during the marinade process. Bring to room temperature (on the kitchen counter) before cooking. Grill or broil on high heat approximately 4 minutes per side for medium rare. Remove to cutting board and top with a few tablespoons of herbed butter reserving the rest to serve with the corn. Cover and allow the meat to rest while the herbed butter melts into it, approximately 10 minutes. Slice thinly on the diagonal and place on a serving platter. Garnish with fresh rosemary and thyme sprigs.

herbed butter

½ cup (1 stick) unsalted butter
1 tablespoon fresh flat leaf parsley, finely chopped
½ teaspoon dried oregano

1 tablespoon fresh basil, finely chopped
½ teaspoon each course salt and course ground pepper

In a small bowl, bring butter to room temperature. Stir together butter, parsley, basil, oregano, salt and pepper. Set aside until ready to use.

Gigi STYLE
FUN & SIMPLE
GOURMET

My Gratitude~

To God,
*for the gift of imagination, and my passion
for all things beautifully delicious.*

To Jeff,
for your inspiration, your love and eternal partnership.

To "The Team"
*To my incredible creative team, I am so blessed that you were all brought
to this project. Your talent and hard work has been such an inspiration.
You have all taught me so much and I am forever grateful.*

Gigi STYLE